SMART MARTHA'S

Catholic Guide for Busy Moms

SMART MARTHA'S
Catholic Guide for Busy Moms

Tami Kiser

Our Sunday Visitor Publishing Division
Our Sunday Visitor, Inc.
Huntington, IN 46750

Copyright © 2010 by Tami Kiser. Published 2010.

15 14 13 12 11 10   1 2 3 4 5 6 7 8 9

ISBN: 978-1-59276-792-2 (Inventory No. T1097)
LCCN: 2010933023

Cover design: Lindsey Riesen
Cover photos: Thinkstock
Interior design: Sherri L. Hoffman
Interior photos: Tami Kiser

PRINTED IN THE UNITED STATES OF AMERICA

✦ ✦ ✦

To all the Smart Marthas God has put in my life: my mom, Kimberly, Ruth, the Aquinas Academy Moms, Paula, my SOC ladies, Denise, Eileen, the moms from OLG Home-school Co-op, and the many Smart Marthas who helped to host my seminars. You all are amazing.

To my best friend: my husband, Keith.

To my kids — Nathaniel, David, Emily, Seth, Michael, John Paul, Joseph, Jacob, and Gabriel — who were the test subjects of the book without even knowing it.

CONTENTS

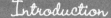
WHO IS SMART MARTHA?

S mart Martha is not a real person. I mean, who would really be bold enough to call herself "Smart"? Definitely not me. I use this term "Smart Martha" as a concept. Someone we can all strive to be like. In reality, I am a not-so-smart Martha — just like the Martha from the story in the Bible (Luke 10:38-42). If you don't know the story, it goes something like this.

Jesus is visiting His friends Mary and Martha, who are sisters. They live in Bethany, not too far from Jerusalem, with their brother Lazarus, of resurrection fame. Jesus has a little crowd with Him, and they are just hanging out. Martha, being the perfect hostess, worries about feeding everyone. She is busy doing the dishes and other hostess duties when she notices that her sister Mary is sitting on her bottom doing nothing, just listening to Jesus speak. Martha is outraged. Who wouldn't be? She marches right up to Jesus and speaks her mind. Expecting Jesus to give her some sympathy, she awaits Jesus' reprimand of Mary — something like, "Mary, can't you see how busy your sister is? Please help her out." But to her shock, the reprimand is directed to her! Jesus corrects Martha for being anxious and worried about many things, and not choosing the better thing to do.

Yes, that's typically me. I am busy and worried about many things — often at the expense of other matters. "But," you may be saying, "how can I be like Mary? I don't have Jesus sitting at my table." *Granted, the incarnate Christ is not sitting there at your table, but Jesus is still there in your home, manifested in different ways.*

One way the Lord is present is sort of mystical — still real, but mysterious: before Jesus ascended to heaven, He promised that He would be with us always (Matthew 28:20). He also promised us that when we are gathered in His name, He is there in our midst (Matthew 18:20).

Another way that Jesus is present, in perhaps a more tangible way, is in other people: He is there as your spouse, as your children, and as any other person God has put into your life. We have examples from

Scripture where we are told that the Lord is present in those around us (see, for example, Galatians 2:20).

A final way that Jesus is present is very tangible and mysterious: His Real Presence in the Eucharist. We find Christ at the Communion table of Mass and waiting for us in the tabernacle of every Catholic church.

We need to be like Mary of Bethany and choose the better part. We need to recognize Jesus in our lives. It may mean having a quiet time for prayer. It may mean attending Mass or Eucharistic Adoration. But it can also mean paying attention to who's at your table, in your car, or in the house next door.

Do you have "Martha" tendencies, too? Are you too busy? Do you forget that Christ is waiting for you, while you consume yourself with all your work? Or maybe you are like the Mary in this story, but to a fault — spending all your time enjoying the company, volunteering at every church activity, while your home is in terrible disorder.

We need the perfect balance of the best of Martha and Mary. *The Smart Martha way is for women who want to get their work done, yet know that their first priority is to look for and always be attentive to Christ, who is present.*

A Smart Martha uses her organization techniques, management skills, and old-fashioned hard work to fulfill her vocation of wife and mother and, at the same time, sees Jesus through, and in, it all. This can mean working hard to get the floor scrubbed. It can mean praying for our family while we fold their clothes. It can mean going on a walk with your spouse. It can mean spending an hour in the Adoration chapel. And it can mean playing a round of Go Fish with your kindergartner! All of these activities can be done while looking for, and seeing, Christ, who is present.

Smart Marthas.

For the past couple of years, I have been traveling to different cities, meeting many women and preaching this lesson that we all need to hear. You've heard of WWJD — What Would Jesus Do? I encourage WWSMD — What Would Smart Martha Do? In the midst of these four-hour seminars that I lead, I spend one part preaching and three parts teaching the practical methods to accomplish all of the tasks that moms need to accomplish these days. And it's a lot of fun! I feel so blessed to have this opportunity, not only because I get to meet so many wonderful women, but also because it forces *me* to focus on the most important thing in my own life: Christ, and Christ manifested through others.

CHILDREN NEED A "MARTHA" MOM

Consider a typical day I had recently. Not only did my kids have the usual piano and violin lessons in the afternoon, but they also had a soccer game and a play practice. On top of this, I still had others who needed a ride home from school. Dinner had to be served — after all, you can't eat pizza *every* night for dinner. Add to the mix a sick 12-year-old. And this was just the after-school time... so forget this "Mary" business! I had too much to do. Besides the obvious time spent in the car, I also had to worry about soccer cleats, music teacher payments, homework to finish, children's Tylenol, and making a salad, among many, many other things. Moms today need to be concerned about "the dishes." How else would our families survive? We all know this — and that is why you are reading this book, isn't it?

This mom business is serious work. Add to that the other work that a woman does. This could be her job, her volunteer work, her care of aging parents, her special-needs child, her work for the parish, her care of her spouse, or her many other demands and needs.

I remember talking to a woman after one of my seminars who had two small children. She seemed amazed that I could get so much done, and wanted me to walk her, minute by minute, through my day. She assumed that I got up at daybreak, scrubbed the floors, did laundry, and cooked everyone breakfast! I told her that nowadays I usually sleep in until almost 7:30, because by then nearly everyone has had his own breakfast and the school kids are just about out the door on their way to school. She was shocked. But I also shared with her that I remembered the days of babies and toddlers. Taking care of them is truly a full-time job. (Mothers of young ones, please don't ever feel that you don't have a lot on your plate. Trust me. It is full!)

These "Martha" tasks that moms have to complete are usually harder work than those of a "regular" full-time job. My neighbor, who has a paid job, told me that she was anxious to get back to work after a maternity leave because she needed a vacation! Moms who take their vocation of motherhood seriously can certainly relate to this. That is why I spend so much time at my seminars sharing tips on how to get these things done and keep order in our lives. Much of this book will do the same. But motherhood is more than just survival! Let's not forget that there are little people involved, and a husband we love.

CHILDREN NEED A "MARY" MOM, TOO

Have you ever had a schedule planned for a busy day? I did. I had it all planned out. This was a day when I was going to be so disciplined and follow my schedule. What joy it would be after following my set schedule for several days when I would have so much accomplished! But it quickly became clear that nobody shared this schedule with the kids. I mean, I showed it to them, but it must not have sunken in, especially with the 2-year-old.

What was he thinking? While I was in the shower, he decided to make another peanut butter toast like the one he had just finished eating. He had learned the very useful skill of sliding chairs around in order to get at whatever he wanted. And although I was glad he didn't bother to toast his bread, he had spread peanut butter not only on the bread, but also on the counter, on the bread bag, and on himself — hair and all! Oh, but wait — a bath wasn't on the schedule for this morning. We all had to quickly get dressed for an errand I had to get done that morning for something I needed in the afternoon. Well, needless to say, I had to change my schedule and take time for the bath.

You could probably top this story. It happens all the time to some degree. That is the nature of children, especially toddlers who can't read the schedule. But hold on — I want to add teenagers to the list. Although they can indeed "read" the schedule, they tend to interpret it in their own creative ways.

It's at times like this that it is obvious we can't take a "Martha-only" approach to parenting. We have to give our children the direct attention that they need. *Our children are the Jesus in our lives.* Like Mary in the Bible story, we need to choose the better part. The dishes can wait while we tend to our children. What I really want to emphasize here is the need to be Mary to our children when it *isn't* as obvious as a greasy peanut butter Mohawk. You know what I mean. You are sitting at your desk reading e-mails when your 8-year-old insists on telling you something about a story he wrote for school. He goes on and on, and you smile and nod your head, although you don't really hear very much about what he is saying. Or you are driving the car, listening to some news story on the radio, while your daughter is telling you some antics about her friend's friend's boyfriend, and again you nod and smile. Or it's 7:00 in the evening and dinner's done and cleaned up. Your 5-year-old wants to play *Candyland.* What do you say? "I am sorry, honey, but I have to finish this last load of laundry"?

Do you get my drift? We all do this far too much. Sure, there are legitimate reasons to have to finish an e-mail or listen to a story on the news or even get a load of laundry done. But we live in a society of Marthas that constantly have to get things done, instead of paying attention to the people who are in our lives. It's the workaholic, industrious American way. Not that there is anything wrong with hard work, but it shouldn't be at the expense of not paying attention to the human beings in our lives. Granted, our society has benefited from all of this hard work. We are very rich, materially speaking. However, I question how wealthy we really are: spiritually, emotionally, and socially. The latter are the things that bring us true happiness.

But enough of preaching platitudes. I am not trying to solve the big problems of society by writing this book. Instead, I am taking a grassroots approach: "Changing the world, one diaper at a time," as seen on a bumper sticker. And I am starting with me, and my family. Won't you join me?

Children, like all human beings, need direct personal interactions with others. They need to be looked at with the eyes of someone who cares deeply for them. Without this, all wither — including YOU! Think about your own experiences. Did you grow up with someone who took the time to play with you, to read to you, and to really listen to you? As a child, you probably took it for granted. But that person was crucial to your personal development.

WE NEED A RELATIONSHIP WITH CHRIST

After reading this, you may be saying to yourself, "Yeah, that's how I want to live with my family." You may make great resolutions to try and live this way. You might succeed for a while — but the fact is, we can only truly live this way when we have a close, intimate relationship with Christ (as our

Mary in the Gospel story did). We always have to look for Christ, as Mary did — otherwise, we just fall back into those same old "Martha" habits.

I know this firsthand, because I have tried and failed many times. I know that I can't do it on my own. I need the grace that comes with a relationship with Christ. I won't cover how to do that in this book. Not because it's not important, but because this topic is so important that it merits its own book. Many fine books have already been written about this subject and are readily available. I am just going to assume that we are all working and praying about this already. A personal prayer life is a necessity if we are going to live like Mary.

But you may be thinking, "We live in such a 'Martha' society, and so much is expected from me. I really do have so much to do." That is true, and that is a major reason why I have written this book: to help women do the "Martha" tasks, but to also have the "Mary" attitude that our husband, children, and friends need. I will try to do this in two ways.

One way is to offer some suggestions on how to make the jobs you have to do for your family easier or less time-consuming. I am hoping that, in this way, more time will be given to those important nurturing needs of loved ones, and less worry for you because everything else is under control. An example of this is to give you advice about keeping the children's toys in order. Having the toys in orderly places means that the tiresome job of constantly picking them up is significantly reduced.

The other way I try to help mothers is by showing how "Martha" tasks can be done with a "Mary" attitude. You see, sometimes we don't have to choose to "be with Jesus" or "do the dishes." For example, I'll make suggestions, such as using "car time" as a time for quality conversation, instead of just getting errands done. Another suggestion is to really enjoy the conversation you are having with your 9-year-old daughter, while you are doing the dishes. We can pray the Rosary, which is a great way to focus on Christ, while we nurse a baby.

Sometimes, however, when we have a tiresome task to do, it is enough to get the job done, and to do it well. Christ is pleased when we do our God-given tasks wholeheartedly. And the best way to do this is to offer them up to Him. Let's face it: *We can do many of our tasks with a "Mary" attitude by paying attention to anyone who is with us; by praying and talking to Christ; by doing them well; and by offering them up.* This is what I mean by always seeking Christ. *This is Smart Martha.* When I use just the term "Martha," I use it to describe only the work or tasks that need to be done.

YOU CAN DO IT, BUT "MY WAYS ARE NOT YOUR WAYS"

Much of this book was written to show you examples of how I do some of my Martha tasks in regards to taking care of children. When a mother starts to take seriously all of the aspects of mothering and tries to do them all well, it can be overwhelming, especially when one sees them all written down.

One point I emphasize to the moms in these seminars is: YOU CAN DO THIS. God has given all of us our own talents and gifts that go along with being mothers. It's a package deal: a baby comes with the means to raise him or her. Sometimes it takes a little... okay, a lot of work. But remember: YOU CAN DO THIS. And sometimes, as many parents know, we feel like we can't do it — that we have failed. This is when we have to turn to prayer. This helps us keep our relationship to God close. If we had all of the answers and everything turned out right every time, pride would overtake us and we would never turn to God. So I guess the emphasis is really: You can do this, WITH GOD'S HELP!

Keeping this point in mind, I also like to tell women that "My ways aren't your ways, and your ways aren't my ways." What do I mean by this? Let's face it: My family is different from yours. My personality is different from yours. My husband's temperament is different from your husband's. On top of that, my children are different from yours. These differences include our hobbies and activities, our finances, our extended families, our careers, and our OCD (obsessive/compulsive disorder) levels — in other words, how much mess and chaos we can tolerate! All of this makes for infinite combinations of differences. I have walked into homes that have seemed immaculately clean, only to hear the hostesses sincerely complain about how messy their homes were. On the other hand, I have had a woman proudly show me her "cleaned out" toy closet, only to think to myself: "I'd hate to think what it looked like when it was a mess."

With this in mind, my suggestions are simply that — just suggestions. You can try it my way and see if it works for you. Chances are, you'll have to tweak it a bit. Perhaps doing it my way will spark your own creativity to see another way that works. Most of the tips I am sharing with you have come about that very way — I see an idea and adapt it to my own situation. If nothing else, I just want you to have the confidence that you can accomplish any task if you just set your mind to do it, and give it a try. Your way may not look like my way — but if it works for you, great!

BABY STEPS

If you ever saw the movie *What About Bob?*, you can appreciate the concept of "baby steps." In the movie, it was the title of a famous psychiatrist's (played by Richard Dreyfuss) best-selling book. It helped the everything-phobic Bob (played by Bill Murray) to overcome his fears. Bob, however, in getting to know his doctor, developed a great relationship with the doctor's wife, son, and daughter. It was the kind of relationship the "all-knowing, well-studied" psychiatrist-husband-dad envied. Bob helped the son learn to dive. He talked to the daughter about her relationship troubles and sang in the kitchen with the wife while doing the dishes. What did Bob know and understand about human relationships that the doctor didn't? What did Bob do differently that received such a great response from the wife and kids? Nothing, except that he simply was a Mary, able to give them the time and pay attention to them and their needs and desires. In addition to remembering Bob, I want to remind us of the idea of baby steps — taking small steps, one at a time.

It's just like the saying, "Rome wasn't built in a day." Or the ancient proverb, "A journey of a thousand miles begins with one step." Some women may get overwhelmed when reading all of these ideas. They want them all, and all of them done — now! Baby steps. Start with one project. "Baby step" your way through it. Begin another one. By the time the children are grown and through college, you may be finished! Just kidding.

Actually, you'll be surprised how much you'll accomplish by just steadily baby-stepping it. Not to be too cliché-ish, but as Aesop has shown us with the tortoise: Slow and steady wins the race.

GO AHEAD AND SHARPEN YOUR SAW!

The fact that you have taken the time to get this Smart Martha book and sit down to read it shows that you have some idea how important it is to "sharpen your saw." This concept came from the great organizer/motivator Stephen Covey. In his book *The 7 Habits of Highly Effective People*, Covey shares the example of a man who has a large amount of wood to cut, and who thinks that he simply cannot take any time off to sharpen his saw. But had the man taken time away from his sawing task to sharpen his saw, he would have finished his job much, much sooner. We, too, often get caught up in the busyness of our days, with the result that we seldom take the time necessary to "sharpen our saw."

Just taking time to see if there are ways to do things better can be a "saw-sharpening" experience. If we decide to have everyone take his shoes off before entering the house, we must then take the time to tell everyone the new "rule," and to follow through as many times as necessary. This saw-sharpening experience will take some time, but it can yield results by helping us cut down on our cleaning. Saw-sharpening experiences can also take the form of spiritual and emotional renewal. If we take time to read, reflect, and pray, then, when we return to our "work" we will have a renewed vision and more energy. I have experienced this when I have taken the time to go to church alone, or to have a childless lunch with a friend, or to even go on a shopping trip to the store by myself.

Deciding when to go ahead and sharpen the saw can be difficult. But if you are feeling dull, or if you can see that a particular sharpening would benefit you greatly, then by all means, "Go ahead and sharpen your saw!"

MORE PARENTING/LIVING ADVICE

Although I may give some suggestions in this book that sound a little like parenting advice, this book is not a child-rearing book. I will pass along some of my experiences, and suggestions, that I hope will help you raise better children — such as, taking time to read to them — but this book is not meant to be taken as a "this is everything you need to raise your children" book. I am a professional organizer (self-proclaimed), and I merely want to give you some practical advice on the managing aspect of having a family. However, my sole reason for helping you to manage your family better is so that you can pay attention to the more important things. I want you to be the Mary who really has a great relationship with her husband and kids.

Along these same lines — and I'm going to sound a little contradictory here — I don't want you to just get your tasks done so that you can go on to the more important things in your life. I have learned this from experience. Smart Martha doesn't say, "As soon as I get my home organized, I will spend more time with my kids." No, I imagine that this is exactly how the Martha in the Bible was living. She probably was thinking, "If only I can get these dishes done, I can then sit down and be with Jesus." I am sure this notion is okay with some things, otherwise we'd never get our work done. But this is no way to live all of the time.

I have spent too much of my life just getting through certain projects so that I can get on with something else. "I can't wait until we get a bigger house.... I can't wait until these kids are out of diapers.... I can't wait until my kids are all in school.... I can't wait until all the kids are out of the house...." With this attitude, you can see that there will always be something else. Your whole life will be spent just looking ahead. I know this is a temptation for young mothers who sometimes feel trapped at home with babies and toddlers. The grass always looks greener. But this is no way to live. No matter what the circumstances are, this is what you have been given in this particular moment. Even if it is a sink full of dishes, wash them while listening to music or an audiobook; or do them with others and enjoy their company; or pray; or just wash the dishes well!

All of life is fuller when it is lived like this. This is another essence of Smart Martha: doing our tasks, but doing them fully present, fully alive, and fully aware of Christ!

WHAT THIS BOOK IS NOT

I've already stated that this is not a child-rearing or child-discipline book. I would not be so bold to write a book like that. I still have children at home. Ten years ago I thought I could write such a book. I obviously did not have any teenagers then. It would have been a Martha-type, control-your-kids book. As any experienced parent knows, control methods may work for a while — even until the kids leave the house. But this is no way to raise human beings — dogs perhaps, but not people.

Maybe 20 years from now, I can revisit that idea and try to tell new parents what it takes. For the present, I am just happy sharing with you some of my 21-plus years of experience in taking care of my children and all their things. If I throw in a little parenting advice, please use with caution!

WHAT ABOUT SINGLE PARENTS, FOSTER PARENTS, OR GRANDPARENTS?

While I'm writing from my own experience as a mother in a two-parent family, this book is really for anyone who is raising children. If you are a single parent or foster parent, many of these tips and ideas will be extremely helpful — and perhaps even more crucial because your situation may require more prayer and more "Mary-ness."

Many grandparents today are taking on a larger role in raising their children's children. And many also realize what a difference grandparents can make in the lives of their grandchildren. For these reasons, if you are a grandparent, I believe that this book will have some helpful advice for you, too.

Chapter 1

TOYS 'R' TAKING US OVER:
Finding Play That Is Purposeful and Manageable

I'm not sure if I have been too engaged in my 5-year-old's play or what, but he really thinks that I want a Batman gun for my birthday. I keep trying to tell him that I like this pretty blouse or those nice earrings, but he seems determined to get me that gun. Even now as I write, I have three Bat Ninja Stars by my computer. (This is breaking one of my rules that you will read about shortly, but there is just something about the baby of the family and getting away with breaking rules.) I mention my situation here because it is a nice introduction to the world of toys. Are they purposeless and a waste of time? What criteria should we use for the toys that our children have? Do we have too many? How can we control them all? Are they taking over our desk area or other areas of the home?

Since toys can cause major disorder in a home, it seems logical to begin our book here. There have been occasions when I have concluded that toys are evil and the bane of my existence. But most of the time, I concede that these nuisances are not only tolerable, but actually beneficial to both the kids and myself. The less important point of toys is that they keep children busy and away from ruining "my" things. The *more important* purpose of toys is that they actually teach children many things. If we have some kind of criteria in mind for our children's playthings, then we can make sure that we are getting the most bang for our buck and bother. When deciding if a particular toy belongs in my house, I simply ask myself this question: Does this toy meet my requirements for play? If it doesn't, and we still keep it, then we are not letting our children get as much benefit as they can from their play.

OUR TOY CRITERIA

To be honest, there have not been too many toys about which I have had to say: "No, this is not very beneficial to you. Let's pitch it." But when it comes to telling the relatives which toys to purchase for our kids, or which toys should be avoided, some criteria have come in handy. For example, there are many girls' toys that I wouldn't allow my daughter to play with — such as certain Barbie-type dolls that I considered immodestly dressed. Boys' toys seem less difficult, unless you have a problem with weapons — then, good luck!

Toys That Engage the Mind in Good Ways

What criterion should we use when deciding which toys belong in our lives? In my view, I like toys that engage the mind. This means that a good toy is one that makes children figure things out or strategize. Or it means that they have to use their imagination. Most baby toys, Legos, blocks, dolls, play kitchens, costumes, cars, action figures, and board games have been the standard toys at my house because of the ways they engage the mind and imagination. The funny thing is, these toys seem to be the ones that can entertain children for hours on end.

(And although this may seem obvious, I want to mention that we must be engaging our children's minds for good. Certain Barbies with sexual appeal or *Grand Theft Auto* may engage the mind, but not necessarily for the good.)

LESS AND ORDERLY

What, then, is the problem? The problem is that our children seem to end up with far too many toys. These toys get mixed together. Pieces get lost. When all this happens, the resulting chaos confuses children and keeps them from playing with the toys.

We may be tempted to think that having more toys results in more play. This is not necessarily the case. I have seen my children play for hours with a simple set of wooden blocks. These same children, when in my friend's "play room," with random bins of toys, got restless after a half hour. My experience has shown me that having fewer toys, which are simply organized, yields maximum play. Think about it for a minute: Isn't this the way most preschools are set up?

Along these same lines, toys that are impossible to keep in order just aren't worth it, even if they are really engaging. I once bought a Discovery Toy Peg "thingamajig" for my children to play with. Like most Discovery Toys, it was mind engaging. However, I can't tell you how many times I had to pick up all those pegs. And even though I spent good money on that toy, I can't tell you how freeing it was to throw that toy away. Toys that cause chaos and frustration for the mom just aren't worth it. Legos, on the other hand, I do keep. These are mostly for the older children, who can keep them picked up. I don't have K'nex or Magnetix. Just the Legos.

It bears repeating that too many different types of toys can be very difficult to keep in order. Certainly, they are harder to pick up and sort if they are all mixed together. Having fewer types of toys helps to keep things orderly. Of course, what one mom can keep in order may be different from another mom. There are many factors involved here. But in general, having fewer toy categories helps the children to play better and to keep the cleanup easier.

So far we have mentioned two criteria for our toy collection. Keeping these in mind can help us decide which toys we want to keep and/or buy for our children and how to keep them in some kind of order:

+ Select those toys that engage the mind for the good.
+ Have fewer toys and fewer types of toys, which then can be easily kept in order.

Can you see how all this is keeping with the Mary/Martha theme? Not only are we concerned about dealing in a practical way with the toys, but we also, and more importantly, want the toys to have a good purpose. If we didn't have this "Mary" portion, we could just buy our children video games and movies and forget about anything else, since they are the easiest "toys" to keep picked up.

THE PLAYROOM SOLUTION

When I was growing up and the kids began to argue or fight or otherwise cause a ruckus, my father would yell: "Take it outside!" Our family didn't have a rumpus room. Today, whenever I hear the term "rumpus room," I can't help but think of a place where kids can wrestle safely without worrying about knocking over the coffee table. Although I don't think your toy room/playroom needs to be a boxing ring, it can keep the rest of the house not only free from wrestling, but also free from toys. I really don't have a problem with kids wrestling on the nicer living room carpet, under Dad's supervision, but keeping those Legos and action figures in one spot can make a big difference.

The playroom doesn't need to be an entire room; but if you have the space, it may be worth it. I envy my northern friends with their roomy basements. Most southerners don't have the luxury of having a basement. A basement has so much potential for great play. I have seen basements with a nice rug for play, comfy furniture, very accessible shelves, pool and ping-pong tables, a "road" painted on the floor for small riding toys and roller blades, swings, and gym rings. There really is no end to what can be done. (Another nice thing about a basement is that you can often just shut the door and both the mess and noise are relatively gone. This comes in very handy for visitors who are just stopping by.)

You can try this line with the kids: "The toys have to stay in the basement. If they come up the stairs, they will disintegrate." Of course, I'd say this in jest to make a memorable game out of it. If the kids insist on forgetting too often, the toys that are found upstairs can "disintegrate" into a box in your closet for a little while.

By keeping the toys in one place, moms are not constantly picking up toys from all over the house. If you do this already, you know what I'm talking about. Just this simple step alone can cut a mother's workload by a fourth. And putting toys away will seem so much quicker if you only have a few feet to walk.

When we first moved to our current house, we did not have a basement, and we did not have an entire room to spare. Seeing the need for a play place for the kids, we remodeled the attached two-car garage into a toy room. We installed a wall of cabinets and bought industrial carpet. At other homes where we lived, we used a sunroom on two different occasions and a walk-in attic for another. In all of these instances, I inexpensively furnished and decorated these rooms. In one of our early homes, I used brightly painted metal industrial shelves, with washbasins as bins. Each bin had a hand-drawn picture of what was inside. I even lowered the shelves, since I had all preschoolers at the time.

Art Expression in the Playroom

Decorating a room like this can be a lot of fun. Did you ever want to paint a wall with splatters? How about handprints? For our garage playroom, we decided on an ocean theme. The walls were painted a medium blue — a good color, by the way, to hide dirty fingerprints on the wall. I hung a fisherman's net with shells and other stuff we had found along the seashore. I even bought art canvasses on sale and let each child paint his or her own ocean picture.

Involving your children in decorating the playroom is a great experience for them. Let them pick out colors and themes. If they are able, let them paint. If kids have ownership of the playroom, they will, "in theory," take better care of it. (I'm not sure if this is really true, but I will take every psychological edge I can get in the "toy battle"!)

As children grow older, and especially into their tweens and teens, having a "playroom" — or now called a "game room" — is important. If your playroom was decorated with fire trucks or princesses and you have someone turning 12, it's time to redecorate. With five teens in our house now, we have tried to make our game room suitable for many ages. It's a playroom by day, often with cars and Legos all over the floor; but by night, it becomes a hangout spot for our older kids and their friends. We decided to put our only television in this room, and attached to that are two popular game systems. In the next chapter, we'll explore the pros and cons of using video games, and how to manage the cons.

Simple Furniture

Before getting too carried away with the walls, I want to stress that it is important to keep the playroom floor sparse. This makes both play and cleanup easier. If the playroom is messy, but without a lot of furniture or other stuff around, cleanup doesn't seem as overwhelming. However, if there are toys everywhere, and the room is cluttered with lots of furniture, a foosball table, a bean bag chair, a game table, a drum set, a dollhouse, etc., kids (and moms and dads) will just look at the mess in despair — and no one will even make an attempt to clean it up.

In our game room, we have a table and a couple of loveseats, along with a stack of sofa cushions that were left over from an old sofa that we pitched. The cushions not only serve as extra seating, but are also great for making forts and playhouses.

A "Playroom" Space

What if you really don't have room to spare for a playroom? No problem. Find a corner or part of another room and designate that as your "play place" or "toy area." For dividers, use cabinets or shelving units that blend in with the rest of the room. This arrangement reminds me of a kindergarten classroom, with a place in a corner that's used for playing with toys.

A rug can also be used to designate the play place, meaning that no toys leave the carpeted area. When the children are all young, and Mom can easily see this carpeted play place from the kitchen, this may actually be better.

Many stores offer matching bins on racks for little toys. These are great to use in a play place.

Toys Elsewhere

There are exceptions to keeping all of the toys in the playroom. When I had at my feet babies and toddlers, who naturally always wanted to be where I was, I often kept a bin of toys just for them in both the kitchen and my office. This special bin was kept in a cabinet in my kitchen, and the other was on a shelf in my office. I could easily rotate the toys to keep these little ones interested. For example, the one bin had a farm set that kept the toddlers engaged for quite some time.

As an aside, it is good to have locks on all of the kitchen cabinets when the toddlers are at the "cleaning out the cabinets" age. I found, however, that instead of buying all of those safety locks and installing them, I could get away with using hair bands or rubber bands on the cabinet knobs to keep them shut. This "cabinet" stage actually lasts a short time — but if you are constantly upset about toddlers getting into your cabinets, it does seem to last too long. Keeping the cabinets off-limits does help to relieve this stress. (Note, however, that I always have one cabinet that the toddler *can* get into. This usually has some plastic containers, a big spoon, some cups, or even pans that the toddler can get out and bang around to "help" Mommy cook in the kitchen.)

If the family consists of children 5 years old and under, then I would suspect that a lot of hanging out could be done in the playroom. Make sure that Mom and Dad have a couple of nice, comfy seats to make this time pleasant for them, or for Grandma when she comes to visit. There is nothing better than a comfy seat when reading to a child.

But what if the family room is not too close to the toy room, and the family with a great age span of children likes to hang out there? Don't the younger children need toys to keep them busy? Yes, this is another exception to the "no toys anywhere else" rule.

Picture a family sitting together in the living room. Mom is reading with the 6-year-old, who is trying to sound out words. The teenage daughter is reading Nancy Drew and the 10-year-old boy and his dad are playing checkers. What an idyllic family scene! I have experienced such bliss at times. But what's missing from this picture? The terrific 2-year-old! Where is he? Is he messing up the checker game? Is he turning the pages too fast when Mom is trying to help his brother read them? Is he demanding that his sister get him a drink?

Definitely yes to all of the above. But what might make this scene a little better is to have a toy bin here for this curious and active toddler. Keeping an attractive basket or something hidden on a shelf filled with toys suitable for his age can help. I've used our Brio wooden toys in a situation like this. I have also used a Matchbox car bin or simple blocks and dominoes. I have even found that having a toy bin like this in the family room works when the family watches a movie together. Some two-year-olds get a little bored halfway through *Old Yeller* and need something else to do. Instead of distracting the whole family, a bin in the family room may solve the problem without the toddler having to haul his own toys there from the playroom or Mom having to miss the movie to go and "entertain" the toddler.

Special, Valuable Toys: Still Another Exception

What if your daughter gets that special Christmas Cinderella Barbie or your son has just built the 2,000-piece Millennium Falcon? Where are these toys kept? Here again I have granted an exception. Especially if there are younger siblings around, there is no reason to frustrate your older children by subjecting their special, valuable toys to being played with by all. When my kids reach age 8 or so, they are allowed to have their own special bin that can be kept in their room. We call it their "treasure box."

All kinds of toys have been stored in these. My oldest son still has his Star Wars action figures in his bin, even though he is finishing up college. My 16-year-old still has his Lord of the Rings figures. My 12-year-old has his Bionicles. I have even seen my children store those very valuable Happy Meal toys. In our game room, I have designated a shelf for models and those special Lego creations. After I get tired of dusting them, I ask if they can join the other Legos. (Sometimes, they have to wait a little while longer, and I am okay with that.)

As far as the treasure box goes, each child is responsible for keeping just enough toys to fit in the bin. Once the bin is too full, he has to purge his collection. Sometimes the toys join the other toys in the game room. Sometimes they are sold or traded with a neighbor, friend, or brother, and sometimes they are just given away. This hasn't caused too much stress for any of my children, and it's a good lesson in keeping order.

With regard to respecting one another's property, I try very hard to be sensitive about this with the older children. They will learn to share and to be generous from your good example, not from being forced to share with toddlers who destroy their toys and their "work." We've remedied this somewhat by having a table in our game room for the kids to play their games on. We all know what happens when a toddler gets his hands on a *Risk* game or *Monopoly* — the toddler is not only at "risk" from swallowing little soldiers or houses, but also at risk of a pounding from the owner of all those soldiers or houses. This table also works for building models, setting up the dollhouse, and working puzzles. To prevent preschoolers and toddlers from messing with toys that can easily be broken, I store all of those toys on higher shelves in the game room.

Putting toys on higher shelves not only prevents little ones from destroying them, but also prevents unnecessary messes. (Have you ever experienced a toddler getting your daughter's beads, your son's Legos, and three board games and dumping them all together on the floor?) Of course, another way to prevent the dumping is to install childproof locks on all of your cabinets.

In the past, when my toddlers wanted to play, I simply opened just one cabinet of toys. This keeps the picking up of toys far simpler. I've even stacked toy boxes on top of one another so that only one toy box could be accessed at a time. This has been particularly helpful when neighbors

A bare table invites games, and keeps them away from the toddlers.

and friends have come over to play. It seems that friends always want to go from one toy to the next, until they have seen all of the options, leaving quite a mess in the process. It took several messes like this for me to figure out that having only so many toys accessible was the key to a minor cleanup — or else just don't ever have anyone over to play... but what fun is that?

A Final Obvious Exception: Bath Toys

You didn't really think I'd suggest keeping bath toys in the playroom, did you? All joking aside, if you have bath toys, have a way of keeping them in order. If you have too many, when you bathe your kids tonight, clean them out. Get rid of the ones that haven't been played with in a while, that just sit, untouched, in the bathwater. If you think they are valuable and worth saving, then try to store them for another time. More than likely, you'd be better off donating them to charity for some other kid to enjoy for a while. Remember, more bath toys aren't necessarily better; but the next time you are at the dollar store, buy some new bath toys to freshen up bath time.

Decide on the container you want for storing bath toys. I used a net bag with a sucker hook for the longest time. This air-dried the toys well, in between baths. When the net bag got old and ratty, I just used a wicker basket. The basket hides all of the toys, and it makes the bathroom look better. But if the net bag is behind a shower curtain, I don't think it would matter. Use whatever you think is best — but just make sure you have a designated container for the bath toys.

The next step is to make sure all of the toys fit into that container. Don't store any toy on the side, no matter how "decorative" it looks. The size of your "bath toy organizer" determines how many bath toys your family is allowed to have. Never more than that. Period.

A "BLANKET SOLUTION" TO NEVER HAVING TO PICK UP TOYS AGAIN!

Having toys with many, many pieces seems inevitable, given that this type of toy often has great play value. I'm thinking of Legos, Duplos, cars, dolls, Playmobil, Brio, and so many other toys. One simple way to pick up all of the pieces is to keep them all on a blanket. When the playing is through, you simply pick up the blanket and store it in a bin. When it is time to play again, you simply pull the blanket out, with all of the pieces still there.

With a baby who definitely is not going to help you pick up the toys, this is an excellent help. Just pick some nesting blocks, baby keys, teethers, and rattles and keep them in a blanket. Lay the blanket out and let the baby play. When the baby or you are moving on to something else, just pick up the blanket and put it away.

The blanket solution is a legitimate way to break the "no toys anywhere else in the house" rule, by simply adding "or anywhere besides this blanket." Just bring the blanket of Duplos into the family room or kitchen for the preschooler to play with, while the rest of the family is busy with other things.

I took this idea to the extreme and made a blanket with a drawstring, which is simple to make. You just need to put a hem around the edge of a blanket. Next, snip off all four corners. Thread one end of the drawstring through each side of the blanket, continuing around so as to make one big circle/square. Coming back to where you started, tie your two ends together. To make the blanket into a bag, just pull on the four exposed drawstrings at every corner, gathering the blanket up into a bag. I have two of these blankets now hanging in my game room on hooks. When my two youngest boys want to play, I ask which blanket they want. They can choose either the Legos or the cars.

A blanket makes cleanup easy.

When they get sick of these two choices, I can either get another blanket or simply switch one out.

I resorted to this system mostly because of Legos. We have such a huge collection, and I was so tired of finding them all over the playroom. With the Legos on the blanket, the kids have a nice selection right in front of them to sort through, which is a lot easier for them to play with.

Cleanup now is such a breeze. We gather the few pieces that wandered off the blanket — including those spaceships that "crash-landed" on the couch — and put them back on the blanket. I pull the drawstrings and simply hang the blanket on its hook. If I have a larger group of children over, I get down two blankets and spread them out in two parts of the room.

TOYS IN ROTATION

I've mentioned that not having too many types of toys is very helpful for kids, not only in their play but also in regards to keeping order. This will be determined by the space you have, the number of children you have, their age range, and which toys you want available for play. You may decide that you will only use these cabinets and/or these shelves and/or these large bins for toys, and that's it. (Initially, of course, it will take a little experimenting to determine what works best. You may want to get more bins, shelves, or cabinets — or more likely, get rid of some toys.) Whatever it is, make a decision — and stick with it.

One idea for a child who has too many toys, but doesn't want to part with them, is to use a rotating toy bin. You simply store a set (or sets) of toys in another place — like the attic. Every few months or so, you simply switch the toys.

Here is how I do it. We have Waffle Blocks (by Little Tykes) and Duplos (by Legos). We also have Lincoln Logs and Wooden Blocks sets. All of these are great toys — except for the many-pieces part — but I have decided that the many pieces are worth it in these cases. What I don't need is all of these building materials out at the same time! After 20 years of boys, I have collected many pieces from all of these collections. Can you imagine if all of these were dumped out at one time? So I use an extra large, round, colorful bucket with rope handles. I dump the Lincoln Logs into this bucket. The other collections are stored in their individual bins with lids, in the attic. I've even used garbage bags for storing the toys that are put into the attic.

Usually at the beginning of a new holiday (like Halloween, Christmas, or Easter — because that is when I'm bringing decorations down from the attic), I switch the bin out for another one. Of course, you can switch them more frequently. I'd like to say that I do, but I honestly don't remember until I am upstairs, getting down my ceramic pumpkins for Halloween. When the different blocks come out, it's like giving my kids a brand-new toy. And this method doesn't have to be used on just blocks or toys with many pieces. It can be used with stuffed animals, toy trucks, board games, and on and on. I've heard of parents doing this shortly after Christmas, when indulgent grandparents have gotten carried away with the gifts. Simply get a box and store some of the toys. In a month or so, it can be almost like Christmas all over again when the toys get switched.

BEWARE THE TOY BOX

When it comes to storing toys in big bins or toy boxes, I strongly warn against using large bins as a catchall. Typically, this is the problem with toy boxes. All of the toys just get thrown into the box and — voilà! — the playroom is clean. But, unfortunately, when it is time to play, the toy the child wants is buried on the bottom. This is frustrating for the child, but even more so for the mom who has to either help dig or, worse, dump the entire box. Furthermore, what eventually happens is that the toys on the bottom get forgotten completely.

The alternative is to use these bigger bins or toy chests for single collections, preferably ones that are made up of larger pieces. We have three other wooden toy boxes, with lids, that also serve as window seats. We keep our Brio collection in one, costumes in another, and the most important bin for a houseful of boys — our toy weapons! The weapons bin, or arsenal, holds about four light sabers, some rifles, pirate swords, space guns, Nerf guns, a Spiderman Web Slinger, and two bows. Our ammunition is running low (mostly lost in the yard) — but for the lucky child who digs deep into the box, an occasional Nerf dart or plastic arrow can be found on the bottom.

Our Favorite Toy Box

The kids enjoy countless hours of creative play with stuff from their costume bin. When my daughter was younger (now 18, at college,

Our costume bin invites creative play.

majoring in musical theater), she spent hours by herself, or with friends, playing this way. Over time, I filled her bin with materials from many trips to the Goodwill store: sequin dresses, old Halloween costumes, fancy shoes, hats, jewelry, etc. We had quite a collection. As she got too old for this, I sadly got rid of the princess dresses, but then went to work on the masculine collection. I always keep a couple of feminine pieces for the few girls who come to visit, but my costume bin now has army fatigues, Indian vests, armor, ninja outfits, and superhero costumes.

Who would have ever thought that this simple collection could provide such entertainment? It is used constantly by my 5-year-old, who dresses up almost every day. Whoever comes over to play with him always goes straight to this bin, and the weapon bin, to choose his attire for the day. When the older kids (my tweens) were on a movie-making spree, this costume bin was invaluable to help create their characters. This is why it is good to have costumes of all genders and sorts. Is this the kind of play

What story will develop with this dastardly crew?

I encourage? You bet! Creative, resourceful, interactive, and reasonably messy. Who knows? Our family may have the next Steven Spielberg, Julie Andrews, or Colin Powell.

"A PLACE FOR EVERYTHING *WANTED*, AND EVERYTHING *WANTED* IN ITS PLACE"

This is one of the mantras I teach when I give my Smart Martha seminars. Notice that it is not just "A place for everything, and everything in its place"; rather, it's "A place for everything *wanted*, and everything *wanted* in its place." This is particularly true when it comes to children's toys. Less is more! It's about KISS: **Keep It Simple, Sweetie.** Only you can make the decisions about which toys to keep and which ones to part with. Use the Smart Martha approach to make these decisions, and keep only those toys that are "wanted."

When deciding which toys to keep, ask yourself these questions:

- ✦ What value does this toy teach my child?
- ✦ What can my child learn from playing with this toy?
- ✦ Does this toy help my child relate to other children and/or adults?
- ✦ Does this toy develop my child's imagination?
- ✦ Does this toy help my child develop fine motor skills or spatial relationships? Does this toy engage my child in role-playing?
- ✦ And finally... is this toy reasonable to manage and easy to clean?

A K'nex Ferris Wheel may meet all of these criteria as far as play value is concerned, but if you don't have a large enough space in your house to build this, then maybe this Ferris wheel is not a good idea. If you don't mind sacrificing the dining room for a while, then go for it!

Before deciding how to store all of the wanted toys, maybe a "clean sweep" is in order. I go over the specific steps for this in Chapter 4. Basically, for your toys, you need to gather them all in one place before starting. You then need to evaluate if every toy is wanted.

Once you have your "wanted" toys, the next step is to decide how to store them. Decide what space you are going to use and what you will use for shelves. Decide what bins you will need. When I am going through a process like this, I always have a pad and pencil handy for writing down what I need to find or purchase.

You don't need to run out and buy everything right away. First, see what you have available. As you have been emptying out toys, you probably have been freeing up bins. What if you have a nice toy box? Great. Think, "What can I store in that?" You can also substitute cardboard boxes until you can purchase something a little more permanent. You may need hooks or shelves. Write it down.

Not everything needs a bin, either. Dolls, trucks, games, and so forth can sit neatly on shelves. I used a shoe organizer — one with those bags that hangs on the back of a door — for Barbies. They work great for action figures, as well. Our aim here is to have a *specific* place for everything wanted.

Everything has a specific place that everyone knows.

The final step, and the most important one, is to make sure everyone knows the places for everything wanted. I've found that the best way to do this is to label. This easy step cuts down on the nagging, complaining, and stress that come when your organizational masterpiece is suddenly in disorder. Simply walk your kids, and your hubby, through the new system — they can't be expected to remember all of the details, no matter how simple, unless you label somehow. You can label something either temporarily or permanently. I have used mailing labels, photos taped on, simple pictures taped on, writing with Sharpies (definitely permanent), writing with pencil, and writing with dry-erase markers. If clear bins are used, then a label may not be necessary. After a while, some of the labeling comes off — but because the kids are used to knowing what's in which bin, they seem to remember. If I see they are forgetting, I just get the labels out again.

A simple test can be given to see if everyone knows where everything goes. Pick a random toy and ask who knows where it goes. Do this until you feel satisfied that everyone — even down to that terrific 2-year-old — knows where everything belongs.

A Very Sharp Saw

Remember the advice in the Introduction about sharpening your saw? Taking the time to "clean sweep" your toys will give you some awesome results. It will bring not only order and cleanliness, but also a better way for your children to play and pick up after themselves.

STORING MESSY GAMES AND PUZZLES

When I was growing up, we played a lot of board games. My mother watched two other girls besides me, and every day when we got home from school, we played board games and watched *Gilligan's Island*. We didn't have a playroom, so my mother stacked all of our board games on the top shelf in a coat closet. It was like *Don't Break the Ice* or *Kerplunk!* to get a game out. And when *Life* would fall our way — look out! We'd have a lot of money and pink and blue pegs to pick up.

For my children, I've tried to make board games a little more accessible. They are in cabinets with shelves, and they are stacked only three high. I like using the original boxes because it is easy to see what is available — and often the game's directions are on the lid. And, yes, I've often had to duct-tape the corners. (As an aside, if you have ever lost directions for a game, they can usually be found online.)

If space is limited, or if the game box is totally messed up, games can be stored in Ziploc storage bags. My checkers, *Candyland*, and *Shoots and Ladders* are kept this way. I have the game boards sitting on the shelf, with the pieces in the bags. This is a great space saver when you can only have a couple of shelves reserved for games. Directions can be taped to the board or stored in the bag. I also store a bingo game in a storage bag. My many decks of cards — like *Uno* and *Old Maid* — are rubber-banded and stored in a plastic bin. You get the idea. Use what works best, and then find a place for it.

The Versatile Ziploc Bag

While we are looking at storage ideas, I want to suggest more uses for Ziploc bags — preferably the freezer ones because they last longer. Instead of puzzle boxes, I use these bags, lining them up in a milk crate that sits on a bookshelf. To store a puzzle in a bag, first have a kid put the puzzle together. Gently flip it over. Take a colored marker and mark every piece; I use dots or lines. Each puzzle needs its own unique mark.

Why take the time to do this? If you have ever found a stray puzzle piece or seen someone dumping a few puzzles out at the same time, you know why. (All the red dotted pieces go in the Tyrannosaurus Rex bag. The purple squiggle pieces go in the Tiger bag. And so on.)

Next, cut out the face of the box that contains the picture of the puzzle. This usually fits just about right into the bag. If it is too big, it can be cut in half or folded.

Since this worked so well for all of my puzzles, I got another basket and filled it with more Ziploc bags, which now store tapes or CDs and their accompanying books. Anymore, the CDs fit into pockets inside the books; but if the pockets get ripped, or if you still have tape cassettes, try this method. This is the same method our library uses with its read-along books.

STILL TOO MANY TOYS

Even after a clean sweep and good resolutions, our toy collection some-how manages to grow. If you don't stay alert to this fact and keep on it, your toys will begin to take over your toy space, and you'll find keeping them in order is again impossible. Jeff Campbell of the Clean Team, in his book *Clutter Control: Putting Your Home on a Diet,* suggests keeping a certain number of items in mind.

For example, let's say that I am only going to have five baby dolls on this shelf. If my daughter gets another baby doll, she will have to give, or store, one away. I've adapted this idea for my storage; but instead of remembering a number, I only use a bin or a certain amount of space.

As another example, I have four shelves for board games. If I can't comfortably fit a board game on this shelf, then it's time to get rid of one of the games. I do the same thing with bins. If my Matchbox car bin is overflowing, then it's time to clean it out. Although I hate to admit it, sometimes I just get a bigger bin. But watch out for this trap, too.

Remember: The bigger the bin, the harder it is to dig through — and the more objects one will have to clean up.

This process of keeping the same amount of toys is really key to keeping the number of toys under control. It is also a key component to cutting down on clutter. You've heard it said: When something comes in, something goes out.

I am not so strict about this with toys as I am with clothes and house decorations. For one thing, it could be that our children are multiplying and growing. As your toddler advances on to older toys, you may still have a baby advancing on to those toddler toys. And then, if you have another child of the opposite sex, the variety is doubled again. Scrutinize and be selective, yes, but don't be stingy just for the sake of efficiency. This is being a Martha.

Toys are about fun and play, not about fretting over or stressing out. Order is important and necessary, but balance is also important. I have seen errors on both sides: moms who are stressed because they seem buried in heaps of mixed-up toys versus moms who have an excessively firm policy of keeping a limited number of toys and arranging them in very strict and obsessively neat order. All I can say is: Be a Smart Martha!

IDEAS FOR GRANDPARENTS AND RELATIVES WHO WANT TO UNDERMINE YOU

I've heard it said that children get along so well with their grandparents because they have a common enemy. What a terrible thing to say — but in some ways, we can all relate. In defense of all grandparents, I just want to say that they love your children dearly and feel restricted in the ways that they can show it. They are probably financially better off than they have ever been before. Maybe they couldn't flood you with every toy you ever wanted when you were growing up, but now it seems they can do that for your children. With that first batch of grandkids, grandparents just pour on the gifts. This "issue" usually gets better with the onset of more grandchildren, but not always. Every family's situation is truly different, but many, many parents complain about overindulgent grandparents.

What can be done? Look on the bright side: This means fewer toys that you have to buy. You can use the money you would have spent on toys to buy your children other things — like furniture, karate lessons, or tennis shoes. But if overgenerosity continues to be a problem, you are going to have to communicate this, either with your parents or — gulp — the parents-in-laws. And please, be as gracious and sensitive as you can possibly be. They really aren't the enemy. Also, if this is going to cause any kind of serious rift because you have unreasonable or insensitive parents or in-laws, then it probably just isn't worth it. Pack the toys away and rotate them. This is pretty easy to do if the grandparents live a distance away.

On the other hand, if you can get your message across with relatively little or no harm done to the relationship, then go for it.

First, begin with a lot of terms like, "I really appreciate your generosity" or "We are so blessed to have you" or "We can't thank you enough." And more importantly, really mean it.

Next, simply explain your dilemma along these lines: "We don't have enough space (time or energy) to deal with too many toys.... It's my experience that Johnny doesn't play as well with so many toys.... We're trying to make things a little simpler.... "

Following that, try asking for their help: "So, to help us do this, could we just get a few toys and maybe some other things that he needs?" I have found that most grandparents actually love suggestions of what little Johnny really likes to play with. Now you just need be prepared to give good suggestions. Here are some ideas that I think have really helped us:

- ✦ Ask for toys that are very high quality and seemingly expensive. Please assure them that one of these is worth 20 other kinds of toys. Brio or Thomas trains, Legos, Playmobil, or other well-crafted toys come to mind. American Girl dolls or their alternatives are other examples.
- ✦ Ask for toys that have educational value: Discovery Toys, books, model rockets, etc.
- ✦ Ask for dance/ballet or music lessons and the paraphernalia that go with them, such as ballet shoes, dance bag, or guitar.
- ✦ Ask for zoo passes, museum passes, movie passes, amusement park tickets, or water park tickets.
- ✦ Ask for craft supplies, such as markers, paper, or paints.
- ✦ Ask for gift certificates to your favorite stores. A potential problem with these is that kids may feel that they have license to spend all of the money on junk toys — which means you are then no better off than you were before. Instead, I steer our children to use the gift certificates for something big/expensive that they have been saving for, like a bike, iPod, or video game. Also, I haven't been shy about using some of the gift certificates on shoes and clothes.

I had this "generosity problem" when my first son was born. At first, it wasn't too bad, because we really didn't have too many toys at the beginning. But three years later, and with three children, I was beginning to feel overwhelmed with toys. I tried putting some away for later use, but we never needed them because someone was always getting more toys for Christmas or a birthday or Easter. I also secretly returned some to the store for refunds, to use the money for diapers. I gave some away. I re-gifted.

Eventually, after a few more years of this, I knew I just had to say something to the grandparents. I remember doing it gradually, with hints now and then around the gifting time. Thankfully, I think they understood. Actually, they were probably tired of it, too.

For now, I'll speak to them on the phone about what someone wants for their birthday. For Christmas, I've been known to write it down for them. This may seem a little presumptuous, almost like handing someone a list and saying: "Here, buy this for me!" But I try to do it in a gracious manner. Since the grandparents know where I'm coming from, it's actually seen as quite helpful.

I certainly wouldn't suggest starting your discussion with the grandparents this way. But, hopefully, you will eventually get to the place where you can be open about what the children really want or need. Here is an abridged version of a letter I used a few Christmases ago:

Dear Granny Bev and Grandpa Fred,

I know you asked me last week about the kids' sizes, so I thought I would write them all down for you and give you the usual suggestions of what the kids are into. Nathaniel is a size ___ and Gabriel is a size ___.

As far as what to get the older three, they would like both clothes and music. Target is a good place for a gift certificate for them. Also, movie passes. Michael would still like a guitar and is saving money for that. JP and Joseph would like a game for the PS2 (we already have ___). Jacob is collecting Spiderman action figures (we have ___) and Spiderman Legos — which we don't have any yet. Gabe likes anything with wheels. We could use a new dump truck for the sandbox. As far as a family gift goes, we would love another zoo membership.

As always, we are not holding you to these suggestions whatsoever! We truly appreciate your generosity, and we know that your love for us is greater than any gift you can give. We are looking forward to seeing you soon for the holidays.

Love,
Tami

STOP AND PLAY WITH YOUR KIDS — IT WILL DO YOU BOTH GOOD

In conclusion, I don't think I've mentioned it enough: *Toys should also be fun!* To be "purposeful" and "orderly" is important, but let's not forget fun. And, usually, these don't have to be mutually exclusive. Engaging the mind and imagination is fun for kids. And sometimes silliness is the result. A little silliness is good. We all need a good laugh. There is something bonding about laughing together.

For this kind of play, I suggest a card game, spoons, with older children. For preschoolers and toddlers, try dressing up and pretending, wrestling and romping, or tickling and giving "raspberries" on tummies.

We all also need some affirmation. I don't think the self-esteem thing can be overdone when a parent does it. Maybe telling kids in a classroom at school that they all are great in math or that everyone is a winner is overdone — but a parent realistically pointing out his child's strengths can never be overdone. For this, play a game of checkers, chess, or other strategy games. And a child can never be told too many times how much parents like her Lego creation, or what a great job he is doing with a puzzle, or how beautiful she is in that princess costume.

Helping our kids to grow into productive, creative, and loving adults is our mission. Really, it's the Mary/Martha thing again. And toys and play are an important part of this. How we provide them with toys and playing opportunities, and even how we join with them in their play, is an important component to this.

Let's not only give our children balance in the toys they receive, but let's be both Martha and Mary when it comes to actually being present in their play. It doesn't mean that we need to dote on, or hover over, them all of the time. Kids actually do need lots of time alone *and* with other children to develop important skills. But we also need to be present at times for those precious laughs together, and for those encouraging words.

We may need to let the dishes sit for a little bit, while, like Mary, we "choose the better part" and play a round of *Candyland*.

Chapter 2

THE MEDIA MONSTER:

Managing Our Technical "Toys" in this Media-Driven Culture

IT HAPPENED TO ME

I had heard stories from mothers whose children had accidentally stumbled upon pornography while surfing the Internet. One of these moms had a son in middle school who was doing a research paper on Michael Jordan. Someone apparently used this popular search figure to stage a pornographic web page. I was appalled. But nothing is below the dirty porn industry that not only caters to young boys to get them hooked, but also entices them to be the subjects. But as a "well-informed" parent, I was doing everything I could to keep my children safe. Or so I thought. After all, we had our computer in a family/public space. I also had the parental controls on the highest level. But as I found out a couple of years ago, this was not enough.

One day, I was looking on my children's computer to see which websites the children were visiting. Instead of checking the history, which can be easily erased, I went to the history option on the parental-control panel that even erasing the history cannot affect. As I was scrolling down, I found three or four highly suspicious web pages. One of the addresses was as obvious as the proverbial NakedWomen.com. I quickly typed in this address and sure enough, there were naked women — and I'm not talking about Greek statues. So much for the parental controls I had installed! Obviously, some porn vendors knew how to get around those protections. I was devastated. Which of my precious boys had been violated? I went back to the history and wrote down the exact date and time of the viewing, as well as some of the other sites that the perpetrator had viewed.

With a house full of boys — at the time, six were capable of doing this — I knew that I would have to do some detective work. My head was spinning with further quandaries. If it was one of the older boys, do I have an addiction on my hands? What if it was one of the middle-school boys? Will I need a further "birds and the bees" talk? What if it was one of my younger boys? Do we have to give him "the talk" in the context of this dirty situation? Is it just healthy curiosity? How do we explain why boys are curious about seeing naked women?

I caught this only a couple of weeks or so after the viewing, so my first step was to place everyone at the time of the perpetration. I had to do this without letting on what I was searching for. I didn't want to arouse suspicion and have the suspects paranoid or covering their tracks. Luckily, I realized that the event happened during the holidays, when the kids were off from school. I also recalled that it happened when my husband, Keith, and I took our five older children to a movie. Needless to say, those five had airtight alibis. We had left our 12-year-old to babysit the younger three. Uh-huh. It must be the 12-year-old, my husband and I both concluded.

Next came the interrogation. Since my husband is a headmaster at a private school, he knows how to question kids. So we brought in the 12-year-old for cross-examination. But we couldn't get a confession. Somehow I believed him, even though the computer evidence didn't seem in his favor.

Well, after I looked again at the history and the log of the websites visited, I noticed that no search engine was involved in any of these sites. In other words, these sites were known, with the addresses typed in. I also noted that the other sites that were visited around the time of the "Naked Women" sites were ones that I had not seen my 12-year-old use. So I questioned the 12-year-old again. I wanted to know who was providing him information about these questionable sites. (I didn't mention specifically what they were.) Suddenly, he remembered something. The teenage neighbor boy had stopped by the house for a while to check if one of our older teens was there. And, yes, he stayed awhile and tinkered on the computer. He had said that he was checking his Facebook page. I verified this with the other kids who had been at home with the 12-year-old. But why hadn't the kids at home noticed what the neighbor boy was doing? Because they were already really into a movie on TV, and the computer was in the next room.

Whew! What a relief! But it was after that episode that I changed some things around my house. I reported those sites to my parental-control providers, and they said that it is impossible to block all of the porn

sites. I had similar problems with a previous parental-co
The porn vendors always seem to be one step ahead. So j

My solution — a very simple one — has been to s
controls (which came with my Windows program) so th.._
sites listed by me can be visited. Search through the parental controls on
Windows, and it will guide you through the easy steps to do this. Then
you know for certain which sites your children can view. No exceptions.
If your children want to visit a website that is not on the list, they will
need your permission first. When a child has to ask for your permission,
it is an automatic "I am being a responsible parent" opportunity to see
what your child is doing on the computer.

The other thing I did was to move the family computer to an even
more public space in the house. For more help to stay one step ahead and
protect your children, visit *www.internetsafety101.org*.

WHO'S AFRAID OF THE BIG, BAD MEDIA?

Well, I am. Sort of. Just by my referring to them as "bad," you can get the
sense that I do not trust the media too much. But that is not to say that
I view all media as "bad."

It's just that from my experience, a lot of it is bad. Let's just say that
I am more than a little skeptical of the media's concern for my children's
well-being, unless they can profit from it. I think this is a healthy suspicion, and one that all parents should have. Presume guilt, until proven
innocent, in regards to the media.

For instance, I thought that cell phones were nothing but trouble.
I vowed five years ago that we'd never get them. But after looking into
it, talking to parents, and doing a trial run, I decided that with proper
supervision, cell phones were okay. (We have five in our family now, and
mine never leaves my side.) I did this same thing with Facebook. At first,
I thought it was evil and simply a way for predators to lure children. But
again, after some research, I found that, with limits, Facebook was also
okay. (I actually have a Facebook page, too.) And the list goes on.

As parents, we really only have two choices when it comes to the
media: take it or leave it. And yes, I do know families that have chosen
to leave it. They live on farms with no TVs. Their children do not have
access to computers, let alone cell phones. There have been times that I
have fantasized about living like that, but I've decided that for my children and me, it is not the better option.

The media, in all of its forms, is here to stay. According a Kaiser Family Foundation report, *Generation M2: Media in the Lives of 8- to 18-Year-Olds* (*www.kff.org/entmedia/8010.cfm*), which came out in 2010, the average time children (ages 8 to 18) spent using the media was 7 hours 38 minutes a day. And when the researchers considered that much of that time was spent "multitasking" — such as listening to an iPod while Facebooking — the report stated that the hours added up to more than 10 a day! The report went on to show how the children's time was divided between different media sources, divisions by age, and so on. It also showed that many children and teens have no restrictions on their time using the media. This is where I think some good parenting needs to take place.

It seems to me that the wise thing here is to "take the media," but to only take what we want. We can take what is good and helpful, while limiting the amount of time spent.

SETTING LIMITATIONS

I am taking a risk here in sharing with you what kind of limitations and rules we have set for our family. I think some readers may be "scandalized." Some may think that I am far too liberal. On the other hand, others will think that I am living isolated "on that farm," far too conservative. And, trust me, I think about both of these positions at times. Keith and I are always asking questions like these: "Do we need some time restrictions on the cell phone? Is our son old enough to have a computer without parental controls?"

I think that sharing what my family does will provide you with the most help. Why? Not because I expect you to do everything like we do, but because it will probably provoke discussions and decisions. It may actually help you to come up with what works best for your family and your situation.

As I said in the Introduction: "My ways are not your ways." Every family is unique. We live in different environments. We have different upbringings. We have different temperaments. It stands to reason that the limitations each family sets will be different.

MARY AND MARTHA IN THE MEDIA

Practically everything I mention in this chapter will be a Mary/Martha approach to media. It may seem like lots of rules and lots of "managing." Deciding where to put the computer, what type of Game Boy to get, or

even where to charge the cell phone may all sound like ?
but behind all of these suggestions is the heart of Mary. ?
given in this chapter are not just about keeping orde?
Instead, they are about helping our children to develop gᵢᵤ.
healthy relationships, and to learn how to properly manage the meᵤᵢₐ
on their own.

Sometimes I will tell you how I use technology to set parental controls — on phones, games, or the computer. But as I've just mentioned, the primary strategy is to be very involved in your children's lives, helping them to make the best decisions on their own. Technology can help us to set controls and to monitor. Unfortunately, many teens have learned how to get around these controls. The only solution to this is to really know our kids.

For help in setting up the latest parental controls, and to learn what is available technology-wise, I often go to Kim Komando's parent section on her web page: _www.komando.com/kids/parent-tips.aspx_. Her articles focus on such issues as "Control the volume to protect kids' hearing" and "What to know before giving kids an iPod touch." I will mention some of the ways I use technology to control and monitor my children's media, but these are far from exhaustive, and definitely not "rebellious, computer-savvy kid-proof."

HELPING OUR CHILDREN MAKE GOOD DECISIONS

One of my favorite children's authors is Chris Van Allsburg. His book *The Wretched Stone* is about a sea captain and his crew who bring aboard a glowing stone that mesmerizes the sailors. They spend hours just starring at this stone. Eventually, the crew becomes useless, as they have all turned into monkeys. The glowing stone, which is only shown from the back, looks suspiciously like a TV. Enough said.

My children understand, in no uncertain terms, how I feel about television. We often discuss its many downfalls. We know from our own experiences how the TV can make us feel lethargic and lazy, focus our attention on bratty behaviors, and most significantly, waste our time. What is important here is that your children know how you feel about the TV. They also need to understand for themselves its potential harm. If we keep these issues in front of our children, we are helping them to make their own decisions, now and in the future. This is much more important than just giving kids a set of rules and telling them to follow them blindly.

Can they be left to make up their own rules to follow? Eventually. But they must always be guided and supervised until they are mature and ready. As our children grow older, this can be one way that a parent can begin to let go. Give the teen freedom regarding some of these decisions, and observe how he does, but always be there to discuss the experience. This is wise, as it prepares that teen for when he finally leaves the nest. Kids need to learn to use their freedom in ways that will make them truly happy, and truly pleasing to God. If college is a teen's first opportunity to taste freedom, then your family might be in for a bumpy ride.

In our family, as our children move into their mid and late teens, we give more freedom regarding movie choices. A few movies have been watched by our older teens that I never would have allowed a couple of years prior to this. Often times, I hear my older teens speaking out against these movies and insisting that the younger siblings not be allowed to see them.

My older three children — now 21, 20, and 19 — very, very seldom see a movie that contains gratuitous sex, even though they know that they have the freedom to do so. Why? It could be because we have discussed with them why watching movies like this are harmful to themselves and their relationships with members of the opposite sex. This is part of a continuing conversation that started long ago when we began talking about dating and sex. Movie selection is a way to keep that conversation going, especially as teenagers get older.

TV RULES RULE!

Back to the "wretched stone." Even though we do discuss with our children why we need limitations, we still insist that certain rules be followed. As mentioned earlier, we make some exceptions with the older teens; but for the most part, these rules apply to all, even to us parents. And even though these limits are open for discussion, this, too, is within reason. Sometimes kids want to argue just for the sake of arguing or just for the sake of getting their own way, not because they want what's best for all. (Imagine that!)

Limit What Is Viewed

First of all, our family decided to do away with cable television. This is not because we think it is wrong for a family to have cable. We just wanted to save a few bucks *and* have a simpler solution to not worrying about watching the wrong channels. I know this decision saved us a lot of hassle. But if you have cable or satellite TV, please block those channels that you know have absolutely no value. Otherwise, just tell the children that they are only allowed to view particular channels of your choosing. (Make your list based on what shows are on these channels. And this list may or may not include the major networks.)

I wouldn't allow channel surfing unless this is your set "TV time," and then only on those channels you allow. Marking the permitted shows in a TV directory every week helps to limit both what is viewed and how much time is spent viewing. Marking these shows together with your kids is also an opportunity to discuss the shows you and your children like, and it also teaches your children how to make these kinds of judgments. Just get out the highlighter and mark up that TV guide. Can your family stick to this? Can you?

We also make our children ask permission before they turn on the TV. If they view television without asking, then they are restricted from the TV for a while. And when they ask for permission, if their request seems reasonable, then, by all means, I let them, mostly as positive reinforcement for asking.

Limit How Much Is Viewed

Almost as important as *what* is viewed is *how much* is viewed. Too many parents seem to think that as long as kids are watching "family" TV, everything is fine. Many parents don't seem to bother limiting how much TV is viewed. After all, their children are behaving themselves and not making any messes. This is very unfortunate for the children, whose childhood risks being lived vicariously through the eyes of Miley Cyrus or Raven-Symoné.

Parents sometimes forget that time is precious for children, too. The childhood opportunities for growth and development, once lost, do not return. Sure, children can learn a few things from TV shows. But after a short while, that learning curve goes flat. The TV can only do so much. Even as a means of entertainment, a lot of television results in children having short attention spans and higher expectations for entertainment. Just ask any veteran kindergarten teacher. She can tell you how children's ability to sit still and concentrate has dramatically declined as children's TV viewing has increased over the years.

But as far as I'm concerned, what really makes this an issue is the wasted time. Even if children are not picking up bad habits and shaky morals, I think that a lot of TV viewing wastes their time. Think of what could be done with all those hours spent passively in front of the TV: time that could be spent playing with other kids, playing by themselves, reading, learning a musical instrument, making an invention, running a business, drawing and painting, writing, practicing a sport, building forts and tree houses, and on and on.

All of my kids are musically inclined. Some are very talented on different instruments. I don't think they would have developed this love of music if they had spent the hours they wanted in front of the TV.

Here's What We Do

So what is our policy? It's simple. First of all, the TV is only on with permission. I let the young kids — who like *Sid, the Science Kid* and *Arthur* — spend up to one hour a day watching educational television. This time limit includes DVDs, as well. Two hours is the recommended daily limit from the American Society of Pediatrics. I just keep track of this myself, reminding the kids how much time they have left. Often it is far less time than this.

As far as the older children are concerned — mostly the teens (those too old for *Arthur* and *Sid*) — they have one or two shows a week that some of them watch. And the kids all know that homework comes first: "If your work is not done, you don't watch."

We make exceptions to the one-hour rule when a program is of interest to the whole family and we can watch it together. We like to watch *Extreme Makeover: Home Edition* or *American Idol* occasionally. We also enjoy the Olympics and other big sporting events.

Older teens — such as my daughter, for instance — like to keep up with the shows that their friends from school watch. And, frankly, most of these shows are not for family viewing. But we have compromised by sticking with two programs a week. Since these are not necessarily family shows, these times have become bonding opportunities twice weekly between older teens and parents. Most of the time, these shows are rated PG; but on certain occasions, there are sexual situations almost making them PG-13. And, no, we don't have to give them a lecture *every* time they see someone getting in bed with someone else. The older teens have heard our view, and we've discussed it and evaluated it.

Some time ago, I saw an article, published in three different newspapers, that reported on a study showing "a prospective link between exposure to sexual content on television and the experience of a pregnancy before the age of 20." Did I cut this article out and put it on the breakfast table for the teenagers to read? You bet! Did we discuss the possible reasons behind this finding? Yes, and this is what we came up with: TV portrays sexual activity as a fun, essential part of dating, with no consequences. So why wouldn't young people have sex? It's as natural as holding hands. After all, this is what TV portrays to teenagers watching these shows. Is this reality? I then mentioned the countless other news reports we've seen about teen suicide, domestic violence, abortion, and unwanted pregnancy. What do these articles all have in common besides miserable people? More often than not, they are miserable people living unchaste lives.

I have heard of parents who have put a little lock on the plug for the TV, to control when their television set is on. We've never had to do this, but there have been times that I hid the remote because I was tired of the children "forgetting" to ask. After all, the easiest thing for a parent to do is to just let the kids watch whenever, and whatever, they want. This may be the easiest, but it isn't the best. I often remind my children of this, and they sometimes reply: "Well, then, just let us watch." But this is when I'm ready with a really great comeback:

> Sometimes what is best is not the easiest. Most of the time it's this way. But because I love you so much, I want what is best for you. A mindless couch potato is not the best for you. That is not what you want. Imagine how good a soccer player you could be if you spent the time practicing instead of watching TV? [Of course, I substitute "piano player," "good student," "making money," etc., depending on my "audience."]

"Using" the TV

The most positive aspect of TV for our family is the time we spend watching together and talking about the shows we watch. Our usual Sunday family tradition is to hang out together during the day; have a late, light supper; pray the Rosary together; and then watch *Extreme Makeover: Home Edition* or an NFL game.

There are times when I have used the TV as a babysitter. This is another way to "use" the TV. Although this has been very helpful at times, it can quickly turn into a bad habit. I watch myself very carefully on this, and always weigh the negative against the positive. If I absolutely have to get some work done, I will use the TV if nothing else seems to be working at the time. And I always use the two-hour limit per day. I also never do this more than once or twice a week.

Let's face it. Sometimes mothers just need a break. We really do. But, again, please be careful here, especially if it happens over and over. What seems to be giving Mother a break can compound the problem. Junior is driving Mommy crazy because he can't just sit and play. By letting him watch his favorite action-packed videos, Mom is able to get some work done. What Mom may not realize is that she may actually be contributing to shortening Junior's attention span and feeding him with a desire for more action — not quiet, concentrated play. Perhaps the little guy needs some detoxification — lots of quiet time and some simple books and blocks with a very caring parent.

I have heard of mothers using tokens or tickets for kids to "win" TV time. This is an interesting idea. Each token can be worth 30 minutes of TV. Children can earn tokens by doing their chores or homework, and can then cash them in when they want to watch TV. This hasn't worked so well for me because I have trouble keeping track of tokens, both in giving them out and in receiving them. I like simple and consistent methods. I did try this once, but wasn't able to stay consistent. Also, because I have multiple children, it was hard to keep everyone from watching those 30 minutes that just the one child had earned.

DVDS, VIDEOS, AND MOVIES

The same rules for TV also apply to DVDs and videos in our house. You need permission to watch them, and I also limit how much time is spent watching them. For the most part, DVD movies are saved for the weekend. We use these movies as our fun, weekend family time, usually Friday or Saturday night. Often my husband and I spend one of these nights with the kids; the other night we go out. To help whoever is babysitting on our night out, I always leave a movie for the children.

Do you have DVDs that you wouldn't want your children to see? Keep these out of sight. For the most part, we try to not even own movies that have scenes in them that children should not view. Those movies are easily accessible from the video store. Why would we take a chance by having them on our shelves? We don't want our children thinking that we have a "dirty little stash of movies" hidden away. Without sounding like hypocrites, we try to explain to our children that some movies

contain too much violence and other images that aren't ⟨
view until they have a little more understanding of the

Watching What We Watch

What criteria do we use for movie viewing? This can sometimes be difficult to determine.

We think every movie needs to be considered individually. The ratings are somewhat helpful, in the sense that anything beyond a G rating needs to be looked into. If it is PG, we'll let our teens see it, unless we've heard other things about it. Take, for example, the film *The Golden Compass*, which was released several years ago. Although it may not contain excessively violent scenes or other questionable images, it may still present a series of stories that don't support the values you want your children to have.

Now PG-13 movies always need to be looked into, even for teens over 13. These films can get away with so much sexual activity and still receive the PG-13 rating. We have, at times, even chosen R movies over PG-13 ones because they were really good movies but happened to slip in the F-word or had some violence.

What is a parent to do? Do we have to preview all of these movies? Luckily for us, no. But screening movies still requires some diligence on our part. There are two websites that we have found helpful: Plugged In Online (*www.PluggedIn.com*) and Screen It (*www.ScreenIt.com*).

Plugged In Online, sponsored by Focus on the Family, gives fair, balanced reviews, mentioning both positive and negative aspects, from the parents' perspective. The problem with this site is that it doesn't have as large a selection as Screen It. I've looked for older movies and haven't been able to find them.

Screen It is very comprehensive, but comes with a $25 yearly membership price. It, too, gives fair, impartial reviews. It simply presents the specific contents, and their contexts, and lets the viewer make the decisions.

In order to monitor what their children watch, parents also need to be aware of when kids are viewing movies elsewhere. Our rule is simple for kids under 17: "Before you watch anything, check with us" (a point in favor of the cell phone). We have had our 7-year-old come home from a friend's house to announce to all that he had just seen a movie I probably wouldn't have permitted. Obviously, he needed to be taught the "ask mom before watching any movie" rule. Sometimes younger kids don't

. told all of the rules. This was the first time it had come up with him. Luckily, it wasn't anything serious.

For our teens, this has been a particularly tough rule to follow — but we have remained consistent on this. I have even checked up on them by getting in touch with the parents at the house where they were watching a DVD. To illustrate: One of the kids calls me at home or on my cell. If I'm not familiar with the film, I go to my computer and visit one of the move-review websites mentioned above. In a matter of a few minutes, I can give them the "yea" or "nay."

Most of the time, the other parents are oblivious to the fact that I may have a problem with the movie:

> "Mrs. _____, this is Tami Kiser. Is my son there?"
>
> "Sure, your 13-year-old is watching *American Pie* with the other boys. I just made them some popcorn."
>
> "Can I speak to him right away, please?"

Just making that phone call once is enough to encourage my teens to either make the phone call every time or skip the movie entirely. Often times they already know that I disapprove of the movie, so they will try to suggest a movie that is a better choice. This is certainly best for all.

Not only does every movie need to be considered individually, but each parent also needs to know his or her child individually as well. What might be okay for one child is not necessarily okay for another child, even if they are the same age. Maturity, gender, faith, stages, and temperament are all factors to be considered. If your 4-year-old is going through a hitting stage, then *Kung Foo Panda* may not be a good choice. Or, on the other hand, maybe it could be a good choice if you wanted to talk about controlling one's temper and the right time to hit someone. (Say, if a Leopard Ninja is threatening your village. Okay, maybe that's a bit of a stretch.)

VIDEO GAMES

I use the term "video game" for any electronic game that is solely for the purpose of entertainment. Such games include those that are played on the TV (such as PlayStation and Wii), handheld games (such as Gameboy and Nintendo DS or PSP), and games that are played on the computer. We currently have all of these game systems. Not that I have bought all of these myself; some were bought by the kids with money from summer jobs and birthdays.

The same cautions about watching too much TV can also be applied to too much video-game playing. My children argue with me that there is a difference, claiming that they are actively involved, having to think and coordinate moves. I will grant them this. But I still have one major argument: in abundance, it still wastes time! And some games — although I don't think any of ours fall into this category — have very violent themes. I can't imagine how someone can spend hours on end hitting and killing people in a game and not have it affect how he or she treats people in real life.

Cautions About Which Games Can Be Played

Perhaps I should first make it clear that the same reasonable movie guidelines should be used for video games. Even though we will allow R-rated movies in our home, we will never allow an M-rated video game. The difference? The allowable R-rated movies are mostly for the older teens. Also, the R-rated words and actions often slip by quickly in these movies, sometimes fast-forwarded over by me. In video games, the R-rated materials are played and heard over and over again — often at the choosing of the player. For example, in one racing video game, players can choose to enter a nightclub with nude dancers. Needless to say, this seems radically different to me.

Sometimes, I will allow a Teen-rated game after a quick evaluation. Often this is determined by the game. For instance, I like the *Lord of the Rings* and *Star Wars* games; I don't have a problem with valiant swordsmen killing Orcs or Clones.

So, how is a parent supposed to judge the appropriateness of a video game? First, talk to your kids. Chances are, they have played the game at someone's house. Again, keep up on what games your kids are playing where. Call the friend's parents if you are unsure. Most kids love to talk about this stuff, so just keep listening.

The guys behind the counter at the video-game store are another information resource. They usually are experts and can probably tell you everything you need to know about what is in the games. (I wouldn't rely on them for age-appropriateness advice, however.)

Finally, pay attention to the manufacturer's information on the package, which states what the game is rated, and why.

However, I have learned from experience that sometimes none of these methods reveal what is really in the games — so get in there yourself and play a few times.

For Christmas, we purchased one of the *Dance Dance Revolution* games, which we had played at a cousin's house once. Everyone had a fun time, so I bought one for us. However, we noticed in our version that there was a music video with song selections that looked like those that would be featured at a "topless bar." Granted, the women did have clothes on, but their outfits looked pretty skimpy to me. Maybe I'm just not used to seeing music videos, and the way the women dress and dance in these. But I don't want to ever get used to this, and I especially don't want my children to get used to it. The *Dance Dance Revolution* game had an E10+ rating. Can you believe it? For children who are 10 and older! I wrote several letters to the Entertainment Software Rating Board (ESRB), which does the ratings, but they assured me that their experts had felt that this was an appropriate rating for this game.

I guess what the "experts" conclude preteens can watch is different from what I think. The lesson here: Don't always trust those ratings!

How Long Should They Play?

Once you have determined what can be played, the next question is how long is too long to play? There will be many factors to be considered when making this decision.

One of these is your child's temperament. We have children who are happy just playing for a little while, then quitting. On the other hand, we have kids who want to play every minute they can; we have to drag them away.

Another factor is how they spend the rest of their time. Do they get their schoolwork done? Are they spending time on their sports, hobbies, or artistic pursuits? Time spent on video games is time that could be spent doing so many other positive things! Have you told your children this enough?

To make this easy for ourselves, we have set certain times that these video games can be played, whether computer or handheld games. Currently, and for the past three years, it has been on Saturdays, after chores are done. Sometimes we play on really rainy days, when chores and schoolwork have been completed. We also permit video gaming in the evenings, if we have special guests over — not the usual friends or neighbors. If we have noticed that a certain child has played for more than an hour, we make him do something else for a while. (Another advantage of a large family is that there are many turns to wait — especially when you

Bins can keep these items easily in order.

factor in that each family member has one or more friends or neighbors who also are waiting to play.)

In the summer, I have made children "earn" their Saturday playing time. They earn 20 minutes of playing time for every hour of reading through the week. When we have had reluctant instrument "practicers," we will count this practice time with their reading time. (After all, they are reading music!) Also, if there are summer math workbooks to do, I will count this toward that time.

Generally, my reluctant readers are the adamant video-game players, so this is the motivation they need. Although it does take a little surveillance, I think this method is definitely worth it. Most of the time, the children keep track of this themselves during the week, trying to read an hour a day. They also keep tabs on the other kids so that they get their fair turn.

Under these simple rules, there can be many advantages of having these video games. I love the fact that my older children get into playing these games with the younger ones. Some games, like *Zelda*, have become family affairs, as we work together trying to beat it. Although I held out a long time before consenting to the Wii, I actually like to see how four players — including adults — can enjoy playing sports games together.

Have you ever tried *Guitar Hero* or *Rock Band*? Jamming with your kids to some Kansas tunes is a lot of fun. After all, many of the songs in these games are from our "older" generation. Sure, Keith and I do prefer classical music — but until they come out with *"Chamber Music Hero,"* with violin, cello, and piano, we'll just have to settle for these rock classics instead!

Keeping Video Games in Order

Up to this point, I haven't written much about organizing all this stuff. But here is another advantage of video games: They aren't very messy, especially if you have a few simple rules for their care.

Store the games in their cases, in one bin, so that the title are showing; or line them up like books. Insist that the games be returned to their cases when they are not in use. We wrap cords around the controllers and set these in a bin, along with the game console. If things get left out, I confiscate the games for a week or make the offender do an extra chore to get them back. This threat motivates the kids to put the games away. It's amazing how quickly they learn this lesson!

Handheld Video Games

Remember that bin of special toys that goes into each child's room? The children who are fortunate enough to have their own handheld game systems store them in those bins. They have to use the games "out in public," with the same video rules already mentioned. The reasons for insisting on a public space while using those individual game systems is twofold: first, the child is not completely alone and isolated from the rest of the family; and second, he or she can be more easily monitored.

One of these handheld game systems, the PSP, has limited wireless Internet access. This means, of course, that some of the dangers of the computer are right there in the palm of the child's hand. There are parental controls that can be applied to the PSP. I couldn't find this on my own. But, luckily, my son who has this game system willingly showed me how to apply them. To access the Internet now, he has to bring the PSP to me, and then I type in a four-digit password. I also have the settings on the game set to a rating of 9. I guess this means that Teen-rated videos and games can be shown, but no adult or mature ones will play.

These complications and extra precautions should be kept in mind when a child receives or purchases one of these handheld game systems. The old Nintendo DS, which does not have Internet access, seems like a safer choice — but now I see that the new one does indeed have limited web access to play with other players. It may or may not have other Internet access. The point, again, is that parents must do their homework and constantly keep updated.

(Here is another tip about those handheld systems. We do allow our children to use these on long trips [over one hour] in the car, as long as they reasonably share with others. Even then, we still set some time limits so they won't play for a straight nine hours on our trip to Grandma's house. Car time can be a valuable time for talking, so we only allow handheld games on these longer trips.)

TVS AND VIDEO GAMES IN THE BEDROOMS

Are you kidding me? Not only would it be very hard to monitor the shows, the games, the movies, and the amount of time spent with these things, but it would mean that any of the positive aspects of watching television and playing games together — our social time, learning to discuss and evaluate — would be completely eliminated. TVs in bedrooms take your children away from you and the rest of the family. Not to mention that it constantly beckons them there, calling them away from their schoolwork, their instrument practice, their reading, and other, more worthwhile pursuits.

TIME SPENT ON THE COMPUTER

Besides very carefully monitoring the Internet, we also need to monitor the time spent playing computer games. We use the same criteria for computer games as we do for video games. What gets a little tricky here is that we have some "educational" games. I put the word "educational" in quotes because some games have far more entertainment value than educational value. This will be up to the parents to decide, but what our family has done is let the kids use what we have deemed "educational" CDs on our family computer. These are kept in a CD binder near the computer. And we pretty much let them have unlimited use of these. (*Sponge Bob Typing*, *Math Blaster*, etc.) We watch, of course, so that no one gets carried away. Again, to simplify our monitoring of this activity, and to save our computers for more important use, we have said no to "uneducational" video games being played on the computer.

If you have computer video games, I suggest that the rules should be the same as they are for the other game systems. Schoolwork always takes precedent on the computer. If someone has research to do or a paper to type, he or she gets priority. With a house full of teens, it isn't unusual to have more than one person working on a paper at the same time. Fortunately, my husband and I can lend our laptops for schoolwork, if necessary.

As tempting as it is to provide everyone with a computer, we have resisted doing this until a child's senior year of high school. Pornography is a serious problem, as mentioned earlier in this chapter, even among the "good kids." According to Norton Online Family (*http://onlinefamilyinfo .norton.com*), a monitoring system offered by the Internet security company Symantec, the top five online searches for children and teens in 2009 were YouTube, Google, Facebook, "sex," and "porn."

At least during the senior year, I can still offer guidance in some small way. Since two of my college-age sons have their own computers, I do worry about pornography. Now, I don't really feel that I should sneak a peek into their computers. Instead, at this point, since they are both young adults, I look for other signs and keep the dialogue very open. (Not that it is too late to still give seniors instruction, but these conversations about the harm of pornography have to begin when adolescence starts.) But, believe me, if I had good reason to suspect pornography use, I would confront the child — and depending on the seriousness of the problem, seek counseling for him. If your teenage son has any problem with pornography, then do him the biggest favor and closely monitor all his computer activity. For help, visit *www.WhoDoesItHurt.com*.

THE NEW SOCIAL NETWORK

Perhaps the biggest problem for teens is that the time they spend on the computer is time spent away from the family. The proper balance between personal/social time and family time can be difficult to achieve. As budding adults, teens are gradually separating themselves from the family. This is healthy and normal. At the same time, they are still a part of the family, and will always need to be. Teens need us just as much as we need them. Some separation is necessary, as it will yield a better bond. This separation from the family is another reason we need to closely monitor how much time any of our children are spending on the computer and with video games.

This separation begins in adolescence, of course, but don't let your children cut you off too much, too soon. This is a good reason to forbid them from having their own computer or TV in their bedrooms.

If your kids already have their own computers, you could perhaps block access to the Internet, except in the family space, and then the computers would be used only for schoolwork. (No movies, please. What about iTunes? Sure.) Whatever the case, I strongly suggest using the strict parental controls that I spoke about earlier. Free roaming on the Internet in the privacy of children's bedrooms is inviting serious trouble, for both boys and girls. If they have their own computers, make sure you are the "administrator," even if your kids can do these operations better than you. This way, you still know what's going on and can always log on to check where in cyberspace your children have been.

Use some common sense as parents, and don't assume that your children would never get into anything bad. I have seen some of the best parents surprised by this.

FACING FACEBOOK

For many teens, it seems that Facebook and iTunes take up most of their computer time. Let's talk about Facebook first.

I certainly don't consider myself an expert on Facebook. Even though I do have my own Facebook account, I often ask for navigating help from one of my sons. For adults, Facebook is a great way to keep up with old schoolmates, friends, and children who are away from home. Many mothers I know have Facebook accounts to keep in touch with their children who are at college. Sharing pictures and news has never been easier. The reason I am not an expert is because I don't spend a lot of time Facebooking. I know that the time spent on Facebook is time that I could be spending with the real "live" people around me, so I limit its use.

Some Facebook Guidelines

How about our children? How much time should they spend on Facebook? When are they old enough to get a Facebook account? What about Twitter? Is Facebook safe? From my own experience, and from what I have heard from countless other mothers, here is some advice:

1. Facebook is for teens only — at least age 13. This is Facebook's own rule. You have to lie if you are younger than this to sign up.
2. Time on Facebook is for weekends and that "downtime" before dinner. During school nights after dinner, it can be used for brief amounts of time to check on assignments, game times, rides, etc. — within reason. It shouldn't be used when there is an opportunity to be around "live" people. Depending on your family's summer situation, for example, if your son or daughter is away from friends, you could limit it to a certain amount of time each day.
3. Mom or Dad has to be one of your teen's Facebook "friends."

4. Allow Facebook only, and with the private settings only. No Twitter for the teens. A mom at one of my seminars reported that her daughter received explicit photos on her Twitter account. Strangers evidently can send photos of themselves with Twitter. This cannot be done on Facebook.

5. Facebook seems relatively safe, if it is monitored. It appears that Facebook is constantly changing its settings and policies. Teens, with parents' "help," should check their privacy settings regularly. Because I am not nearly as computer-savvy as my children are, I ask them to show me that they have "relatively safe" privacy settings. This way I can learn about the different settings, as well as engage in those conversations about why privacy is important. Like all other media, your child's Facebook needs to be looked over regularly for content and use. Being one of their "friends" makes this easy. If your kids know that you are checking their account, this will help them to be selective regarding whom they pick to be their "friends," and what type of language they use in their entries.

6. It must be stressed over and over again that "what goes online, stays online." Our teens must learn to be responsible for everything they write or every picture they are in. Entries can come back to haunt them.

7. If gossip or negative comments about other people seem to be a problem for the teen, then the teen's Facebook should be shut down for a while.

Facebook Horror Stories

We all may remember the MySpace story a couple of years ago. A teen was so hurt by what someone had written on her MySpace page that she ended up committing suicide over the incident. Does this kind of hurtful gossip happen between some of your teen's friends on their Facebooks? To some degree, it probably does. Facebook makes it so easy to vent your feelings and to say those hurtful things that one would never say to someone's face. My husband, who is the administrator of a Catholic middle school and high school, tells me that every year for the past three years they have had "Facebook problems." You can probably guess correctly which school group is having the problems. It's those middle-school girls. Keith calls it, "Mean Girl Facebooking." This is another good reason to put off Facebook until a later age, when kids are more mature.

DO YOU YOUTUBE TOO MUCH?

I hope we don't. Sometimes I do worry. My son Michael uses YouTube to learn how to play certain songs on his guitar. John Paul, my drummer, watches drum solos. I am convinced that you can learn almost anything on YouTube. Look there first the next time you want to learn how to clean a fish, make a hovercraft, or braid hair. As a dance instructor at our Catholic school, I often use YouTube to brush up on my knowledge of waltz turns, swing steps, and contra dance moves.

Where YouTube turns into wasting time comes when we start viewing too many of those highly entertaining videos. And they are very funny at times. I enjoy watching some of these with my older children. Harmful? Usually not. I've seen some options for potentially pornographic ones, which we have stayed far away from, and I've seen some borderline obscene and crude ones.

I think my children know that their YouTube privileges are in direct proportion to what type of videos they spend their time watching. Since our computer is in a public space, everyone knows what is being watched on YouTube. This really prohibits anyone from watching something slightly profane or violent.

Our recreational viewing of YouTube is a weekend event. It has the same rules as watching DVDs or playing video games. Here are a few of our family favorites, identified by the following keywords: Timewarp (water balloon, drummer, etc.), Will It Blend?, Mentos and Diet Coke, HaHaHa, Rube Goldberg Machines.

(A warning for those of you who haven't YouTubed very much. There seems to be a lot of gratuitous, although very fake looking, violence. For this reason, trustworthy teens are the only ones who should be allowed to be the operators, and they are only allowed that privilege as long as they show appropriate videos.)

"HELLO... HELLO... ANYBODY HOME?" — THE MUSIC IN OUR EARS

I often recall a similar question from an old Pink Floyd song when I see my children plugged into their iPods. When we were in high school, we had our Sony Walkmans. These were bulky and limited to our current cassette-tape collection. Today, kids have access to any music they want, and it's all totally portable. Simply amazing!

If your children are old enough to manage their own MP3 player or iPod, then you have yet another opportunity to help your kids use a piece of today's technology wisely. (I use the terms "iPod" and "MP3 player" inter-changeably.) Think of these devices as wonderful aids that force us to stay involved with our children, and which give us a view into their world.

Now, I wouldn't push this technology on my children. Better to wait until they are able to manage it on their own. In other words, they will have to read the directions and figure out how the device works, or have a friend who can help them. This is usually in fifth or sixth grade. If you can put it off until later, certainly do so.

Managing Our Music

Do we need guidelines and rules for music, too? Yes, indeed. But again, we are parenting our children to help them make good deci-sions on their own. If you know your children and converse with them regularly about music, then you are well on your way to helping them self-monitor what they listen to. Older brothers and sisters can help tre-mendously in developing the musical likes and dislikes of their younger siblings. Take the time and effort to establish reasonable guidelines for the older children, and you will see these passed down to the rest of the children. If I question something a middle child is listening to, I simply have to ask the older son what he thinks of the music. If he says it is trash, then it is removed from the iPod account and taken off the iPod. Parents also affect the standard of music by what they listen to on the radio, at home or in the car. Don't be afraid to turn off a song that is really offensive to you, and tell your children why you did.

Is This Music Trash?

What is trash? Can one person's trash be another person's treasure? Not really, but we all probably have a varying definition of trash. I pretty much assume that most — though certainly not all — secular rap is trash. And since none of my children really like rap, I've had this pretty easy. If they did, then I'd be asking for the lyrics and ruling out many of the rap groups and picking those groups whose lyrics seem fine. And don't accept the baloney that "we don't really listen to the words." The words affect us whether we acknowledge it or not, especially if we are singing them over and over again.

I have a son who used to like some heavy metal. I am fortunate that he also took his faith rather seriously and avoided the songs that had satanic messages. He went through the songs on his own and only listened to the ones that didn't blaspheme his Lord or present him with unchristian morals.

This is the advantage of an MP3 or iPod. When my generation was growing up, we were stuck with the whole album. We were also stuck with whatever songs were playing on the radio. Now our kids can pick and choose the good songs from many different artists to add to their playlist. There is so much music out there that we don't have to settle for *any* questionable songs or any trashy radio stations. My heavy metal fan has since moved on to better music, as often happens with teenage boys.

Check your sons' and daughters' playlists regularly. This is easy to do. In our case, their iPod accounts are on the family computer. These accounts contain all of the songs they have downloaded to their iPods. Usually, our kids love to keep us old fogies up to snuff. Borrow their iPod the next time you go to the gym or on a walk. (They may make you use your own headphones so that you don't get theirs all sweaty!) Take this opportunity to scroll through their music. You'll get a sense of what they are listening to.

Too Much of a Good Thing

Besides keeping up with what our kids are listening to, we want to make sure that they aren't missing out on what's really happening "out there" with real live human beings. In our car, if the iPod is on, it is plugged in so that everyone is listening to the same music and conversation can still happen. If your car doesn't come with an iPod player, but still has a cassette player, you can get an inexpensive adapter. If it's a long trip, we will make an exception to let everyone do his own listening for part of the time.

We *don't* tolerate iPods when we are doing something together as a family. At mealtimes, during visits, or at a baseball game, for example, headphones are off-limits. This is a matter of manners. It is rude to shut yourself off from people who are in your presence. If your son and daughter pop on their headphones when their grandparents come over to visit, then we have no one else to blame but ourselves.

Self-Organizing

Another bonus about iPods is how much clutter they prevent. I remember having my record collection of 45's. Then, I moved on to albums and some cassettes. I had to keep these in big crates. Next came the CDs, which I still currently have; these take up quite a bit of space in their plastic cases. My husband, Keith, still has his music collection in this format. I have since put my CDs into a CD album. It still amazes me that I can store hundreds of CDs in the space of one large binder. I recommend these albums for any and all CDs — both computer and music.

My kids in middle school are skipping the CDs all together. They simply have music on their iPods and on the computer (which is how the music is put on the iPod). No album or CD clutter for this generation!

CELL PHONES: THE BEST, AND THE WORST, TECHNOLOGY AVAILABLE TO KIDS

Cell phones. Both Keith and I are always debating the value of these gadgets. Sometimes the frustration becomes so great that we are willing — at least for a few moments — to go off them, cold turkey. But when we face reality, we know it would be extremely difficult to go back to a cell phone-free existence. A lot of our problems have come from being surprised by unexpected charges on our monthly bill. It took a few costly mistakes for my children to realize how a "free" trial can cost money, and that voice mail can count toward our minutes.

Fueling Relationship Problems and Missing Life

The more serious problems center around the extra drama and relationship problems extended by cell phones. Teens talking on their cell phones late into the night, when they're tired and not in complete control of their emotions, just exacerbates their relationship problems. Things are too easily said late at night, and when we are not face-to-face. We've seen this happen with our older children, and we are determined to protect our younger children from these problems.

Another issue: I wonder how much learning can be done when studying is interrupted every five minutes by a new text message. I've been near my son's room when he was supposed to be studying, only to hear his phone go off every two or three minutes. But he wouldn't pick it up to say "Hi." No, he would simply text back. Keith and I decided that this was crazy, too.

So besides fueling unnecessary or unhealthy relationships, and wasting time that should be spent doing something productive, I also have a problem with too many people missing out on real life because of cell phones. I have a photo of my husband and two of our teenagers on a trip we took to New York City. There we were, standing in the exciting and full-of-life Times Square. Keith is looking up at all the lights and billboards. My children? They are busy texting! I thought to myself, "This is pathetic." In my kids' defense, I will say that they were just informing their friends of their arrival in the Big Apple, and being at Times Square.

But the photo still looks pathetic.

Boundaries and Rules for Cell Phones

We are still working on what really works best for our family in regards to cell phones.

First, we have decided that our middle schoolers don't really need them. This will come as a shock to many readers. In fact, I know that many parents give cell phones to elementary-age students. I understand that for safety reasons and for rides home, cell phones are a great help. But when I saw our 10-year-old neighbor girl with the cell phone plastered to her ear the whole time I was with the children at the neighborhood pool, it confirmed for me that this is not what I want for my kids. If safety is a concern, then a cell phone could be used for only emergencies. I know they make cell phones for children that only dial out and receive certain numbers. And pay-by-the-minute phones are also available.

As far as middle schoolers are concerned, if you would like your son or daughter to postpone romantic relationships until later in life when they are more mature, then don't even think about getting them a cell phone. Why put this relationship tool/weapon in their hands? As your child enters ninth grade, and if he or she seems to have priorities in order, then a cell phone could be considered, especially if this responsible child has many activities. If you have a social butterfly who has his or her nose in everyone's business, then I'd wait until a grade later. What you decide will depend upon the temperament and needs of each individual child.

Cell phone rules for high schoolers? We decided that during the school year, on school nights, cell phones are to be off after dinner until the homework is done. After that, on school nights we confiscate them at 10:00 p.m. I don't know if many parents realize how late at night their sons or daughters are sending or receiving text messages. "Parking spots" at a recharging station could be the norm every weekday night. Many phones now come with parental-control options that turn their children's phones off at whatever time the parents set.

For our family, weekends and summers are pretty free. If a child is having problems with getting schoolwork completed, then we may have to confiscate the cell phone during the entire week. When our kids are seniors in high school, we give them complete freedom. But again, if this freedom causes them to get behind in schoolwork, or causes relationship problems, we may shut off the phone until we have the situation turned around.

Snooping Out Danger

Cell phone bills can be very helpful in monitoring what your kids are doing with their cell phones. They spell out everything. It doesn't hurt to take a look occasionally at how much time, when, and with whom your children are talking to on the phone.

Does this seem snoopy? It does to me a little bit, but I am the owner of the phones. I also let my children know that I am checking on whom they are talking to. If they know this in advance, it isn't really snooping. If you ever have a situation where your child is in a bad relationship, this information could help you know that you have a problem on your hands. Drug dealing? Possessive girlfriend? (One who calls continuously every other minute throughout the night.) Abusive boyfriend? Dial-up sex? Inappropriate relationship with an adult? (What adult calls a child past 10:00 p.m., or has lengthy conversations with a teen?)

And speaking of dial-up sex: Pornography viewed on cell phones is fast becoming a serious problem among teenage boys. Boys can view the raunchiest sites in private, pretty much whenever and wherever they want. All phones with video or photos on them have this access. Many parents may want to opt for phones without video or pictures, especially for boys. This will be one less opportunity for temptation that they will have to battle. This is even a more serious problem with phones like the iPhone or Android, with great graphics and easy Internet access. (To iPhone's credit, Apple's CEO, Steve Jobs, said shortly after the release of the iPhone 4 that Apple has *a moral responsibility to keep porn off the iPhone*. This is great news for parents! I hope other phone companies will follow suit.) Parents who indulge their kids with this technology need to be extra, extra vigilant — checking the history regularly.

If we have girls, does that mean we don't have to worry about problems like this? Of course not. We know of cases of girls sending naked pictures of themselves and their friends to where guys were. Yuck. What a tragedy.

And while we are on a yucky subject, how about "sexting"? This is like phone sex, with pictures and messages instead. Having phones with no pictures can avoid the temptation of getting started with this. But just choosing the right cell phone won't cure this huge problem.

Can parents know if a child is sexting? If it is between "friends," then they will have no way of knowing by just looking at the cell phone bill. I think that a child involved in "sexting" would have many other clues that a parent could look for, like excessive privacy needs and other pornography outlets.

Keeping Track of Our Kids

Another way that technology has worked for the good is that cell phones are great for keeping track of our kids. It makes it very easy for them to call us when they have a change of plans and a change of location. This is one of our more important rules: "We need to know where you are at all times." If they go somewhere other than where we expect them, they are to give us a call.

As kids begin to drive themselves around and hang out with other kids who drive, cell phones have made it easy for us to know where they are. They really don't have an excuse. Middle schoolers aren't quite as mobile, so I don't think this is a reason for them to get cell phones. Besides, they can just borrow one of their friends' cell phones — or heaven forbid, actually use a landline if this situation occurs.

I also love having a cell phone when my younger children are being babysat. It is such a reassurance to know that we can be contacted on the spot if there is any problem. I make sure that all of my children know my cell phone number, and know how to contact me, by the time they are 5 or 6 years old.

Cell Phone Organization and Backup

This brings us to a couple of organizational matters. One is just having a set place to recharge your phones. A parking station, as I mentioned earlier, is great for the children's cell phones. I personally keep my charger beside my bed so that not only is my phone recharging at night, but I also have quick access to emergency incoming or outgoing phone calls.

Another organizational matter deals with keeping an extra record of your spouse's and children's cell phone numbers. Have you ever had a dead or lost cell phone and needed to contact someone, but wasn't able to because you couldn't retrieve the number? This is especially trouble-some when you are trying to get in contact with one of your children. So I keep everyone's cell phone numbers on an index card tucked away in my purse. I also have this list posted on our bulletin board at home. By the way, this is a good reason to suggest that your children — the young ones *and* those with cell phones — should memorize your cell phone number. You never know when the older kids' cell phones may lose power, get lost, or get broken.

Have you ever heard of ICE? This is a campaign started by emergency workers that encourages everyone with a cell phone to put into his or her contact list an emergency contact phone number under the name "ICE." ICE stands for "In Case of Emergency." This is to help emergency workers contact your spouse, or whomever you list as the emergency contact, in the unfortunate event of you being in an accident and unconscious. My new phone came with this already labeled. Put yourself as the ICE contact in your children's cell phones.

Think about it. This is the quickest way to inform anyone regarding whom to contact in this unfortunate circumstance.

The Absolute Best Part of Cell Phones

One final positive note about cell phones is how they facilitate keeping in contact with children who have gone off to college. When I went to college, most students made a weekly call to their parents. Now I can talk to my sons and daughter on a whim. If I am waiting somewhere, I often give one of them a call or text to see how they are doing.

They do the same for me. My son called me once to find out how to make spaghetti sauce. I think that this is incredible — four states away and still able to give some motherly advice!

BE VIGILANT

My final advice of this "Big, Bad Media" chapter is to stay vigilant. Media keep us connected to the world, but these technologies can also distance us from everyone. We know that children need interaction and relationships with real people. We parents need to be vigilant about the time our children spend on electronics, and with the media, so that these things don't take our children away from those real life relationships with the people in our home and neighborhood.

In addition, many theologians and pastors are warning us that the upcoming generation doesn't know how to be silent. And if we are never silent, we cannot hear God. Our modern-day technology is tuning out the next generation's vocation calls. We need to be vigilant so that our children can also learn how to be silent.

Our Blessed Mother and a broken-winged St. Michael on our family computer remind us of their protection — and our responsibility.

Finally, we need to be vigilant about the serious harms that can come from the media, including, but not limited to, pornography. With the iTouch, iPad, and so many cell phones having Internet access, it soon will be virtually impossible to always monitor our children's access to the Internet. We really need to teach our children well!

My husband and I say the Prayer to St. Michael the Archangel every night before bed, with the specific intention of keeping the devil, as expressed in pornography (Satan is master of that industry), out of our home and our children's lives. Evil can so easily be invited in through our computers and phones, and even the neighbors' computers and phones, that we need all the help we can get to battle this plague. We also keep a picture of the Blessed Virgin Mary on our computer as a reminder for us to stay close to Jesus in all that we do. Our children know that sacred images don't ward off evil in and of themselves — like a voodoo charm — but instead represent the holy ones' protection of our home brought about by our many prayers and our devotion to them.

On Sunday, April 24, 1994, Pope John Paul II recommended that the St. Michael prayer be used by all Catholics as a prayer for the Church:

> May prayer strengthen us for the spiritual battle we are told about in the Letter to the Ephesians, "Draw strength from the Lord

his mighty power" (Ephesians 6:10). The Book of Revela-
s to this same battle recalling before our eyes the image
chael the Archangel (Revelation 12:7). Pope Leo XIII cer-
ad a very vivid recollection of this scene when, at the end
oʃ · last century, he introduced a special prayer to St. Michael
throughout the Church. "St. Michael the Archangel defend us in
battle, be our safeguard against the wickedness and snares of the
devil." Although today this prayer is no longer recited at the end of
Mass, *I ask everyone not to forget it, and to recite it to obtain help in the
battle against the forces of darkness and against the spirit of this world.*
(Pope John Paul II, *Regina Caeli*, April 24, 1994; see *http://www.ewtn
.com/expert/answers/st_michael_prayer.htm*; emphasis added.)

✦ ✦ ✦

PRAYER TO ST. MICHAEL THE ARCHANGEL
St. Michael the Archangel,
defend us in battle.
Be our protection against the wickedness
and snares of the devil.
May God rebuke him, we humbly pray,
and do you, O Prince of the Heavenly Host,
by the power of God
cast into hell Satan
and all the evil spirits
who wander the world
seeking the ruin of souls.
Amen.

Chapter 3

DINNER:

Getting the Food and Everyone to the Table to Feed Body and Soul

A MARTHA NIGHTMARE

I have a few memories of dinner together when our family was young. Much of this time is a blur to me. Nathaniel, the firstborn, was 3. David was 2. Emily was 1. And yes, Seth, our fourth child, was 3 months old. We were living in our second rental, which actually had a dining room. Swelling with pride from our new place, Keith and I decided to have two of his buddies over for dinner. Neither of them had children.

The main course of dinner actually went pretty well. We had a booster seat on one chair, two high chairs on the corners, and Seth in the baby seat in the corner of the room. Everyone seemed happy and engaged.

Chocolate!

I proudly brought in dessert: a chocolate cake with chocolate icing. I served everyone a piece, even the little ones. Being the "expert" mother and host, I served Nathaniel and David small "sample-sized" pieces. I gave Emily even smaller pieces on her tray to work on. After all, too much chocolate and sweets are not good for little ones....

When everyone was just about finished, I went into the kitchen to clear the sink a little so that we would have room for all of the dirty dishes. I was such a Martha, always worried about the dishes and chores. When I came back out a few minutes later, I couldn't believe it. Not only was more cake served to *everyone* at the table, but all of the Kiser children also seemed to be wearing it! This wasn't just a little mess around their mouths, but in their hair, on their ears, and on their arms. And everyone was laughing, except me.

It seemed that our brilliant 1-year-old could put her finger on different body parts when asked. So when Daddy asked her where her nose was, she put a cake-covered finger on her nose. Daddy's buddies caught on to the game and asked her where her hair was. She obliged with more cake being left in her hair.

Of course, the fun began. With even messier hands, now on purpose, the two boys had to join in the game with more body-part identification, including tricky ones like elbow and eyebrow. Everyone was howling. Now, a good sport, Mary-like mother could have joined in the fun — but unfortunately, that was not me. I just got mad and confiscated all of the cake, and began cleaning up the mess.

I think I have come a long way since then. Now I serve much bigger pieces of cake to all. And although I certainly wouldn't appreciate the mess, I sincerely think I would join in the fun — but also engage everyone in the cleanup, especially the childless buddies!

THERE'S SOMETHING ABOUT DINNER

When we want to converse with friends, celebrate a special occasion, or simply hang out together, why do we gather around a table with food? There's just something about eating together. Dinner is crucial to the family experience. Often, if we think about family and home, we picture a dinner scenario. It's the most natural thing to do when special guests arrive; we invite them to a meal. Having a meal together is like having them be a part of our family. I really believe that it is something that is part of our humanity. It is the same from culture to culture. It seems to be inborn — or rather, we were created that way.

I don't believe that God saw that humans enjoyed eating together and then decided, "Hey, I think the way that I will have communion with them is by way of a meal." No, it was the other way around. He built in us the desire to share in fellowship with one another through our meals so that we could have that communion with Him during Mass. Not only does our dinner build communion and fellowship with others, but it also gives us the desire to have communion and fellowship with Christ.

Remember, that's what the Mass is: a communion, a meal, and we receive Jesus in Holy Communion. But it doesn't end there. Our image that God gives us of heaven is a banquet, a huge dinner party, a wedding reception (Revelation 19). The family meal goes on into eternity.

With this in mind, it seems rather tragic that family dinners are becoming obsolete in our culture. Soccer practice, working-overtime dads, worn-out moms, teens on cell phones with homework to do, and

TV shows are some popular reasons the family dinner is disappearing. Understanding that mealtime seems to be part of our humanity helps to explain some of the many benefits that come as a result of eating meals together. There have been well-publicized studies showing the correlation of drug use and teenage pregnancy to families that seldom or never eat meals together (see, for example, the "back-to-school" National Survey of American Attitudes on Substance Abuse XIV: Teens and Parents, by the National Center on Addiction and Substance Abuse at Columbia University; press release (August 26, 2009) at *http://www.casacolumbia .org/templates/PressReleases.aspx?articleid=566&zoneid=66*).

There are also studies showing that children get better grades when dinner with family is a regular part of their routine.

Reflecting on my own experiences of dinner with my family, now with hubby and nine children, I think that dinner together can be considered an "application" of the glue that holds our family together. It is not the glue itself, but it helps apply the glue to our family. We'll call the glue "love," because that is really what I am talking about. And dinnertime is what helps keep some of that glue in place.

DINNER APPLIES THE GLUE

Here are some ways that I see this. First of all, there is just taking the time to be together. There is a lot to be said for "quality" time together, but we all know that "quality" time doesn't happen unless we have plenty of "quantity" time. Regular dinners together provide an opportunity to have a "quantity" of time together every single day.

Secondly, dinnertime helps us to build relationships with one another through normal conversations that help us get to know and support one another. Just talking with one another — about likes and dislikes, interests and hobbies, friends and foes, opinions on a multitude of topics — helps to build better family bonds.

And finally, the regular repetition of this ritual helps our family to develop a sense of unity and belonging. "I am here where I belong, and people really care that I am here."

RESTORING DINNERTIME

Realizing how crucial it is for our families, any effort we can make to restore dinnertime to a place of importance in the family will be worth it. Here are three ways moms can improve this: (1) we may need to work toward getting everyone to dinner together; (2) we may need to do a better job serving and cooking the dinner; and (3) we may need to pay better attention to how we use the time while we are gathered together for dinner.

1. Getting Folks to the Table

Getting everyone to the table is a major challenge in our culture. We are all so busy. We live in a society that is pushing us to be more productive at work, to do more activities, and then to make our kids be more productive and do more activities. This combination keeps us in our minivans all afternoon and into the evening.

For the sake of family life, we all could afford a little more simplicity. Less is more. If we want *more* for our family, then we need to see if we can have "*less*" of those activities. I will write later (Chapter 5) how to decide what needs to go and what should stay. For now, let's just try to lighten our load that burdens us around dinnertime.

Have a Set Dinnertime

One way we can help everyone make better decisions is to have a set dinnertime — 5:30 or 6:00 or 7:00 — whatever fits your schedule best.

Getting everyone to the table is a challenge.

This helps us when the kids are out playing or at the neighbor's house. It makes gathering everyone home that much easier. If we know that we have an activity on one or two nights a week that pushes us later, then we change the schedule just for those days (for example, dinner is at 5:00 on Mondays, Wednesdays, and Friday, and at 6:30 on Thursdays). If it happens just on occasion, I make that announcement in the morning to everyone or when they come home from school ("We will have dinner at 7:30 tonight because of the volleyball game").

Will we always be able to do this? No, we have many occasions when not everyone is home for dinner, even after the best efforts. So we just dine at the usual time without them. This usually happens a couple of nights a week during a sport season, which usually ends in a month or two. If it continues on through the next sport season and happens more than once or twice a week, I might see if I can do dinner later or change something else. Every family's situation is different. Pray about it, really.

Another problem with maintaining that set dinnertime is the late-working dad. I have heard from many mothers about this problem. If dad is always coming home after 7:00, I suggest moving dinner to 7:30 or even 8:00. This is very doable if the kids are older or have the ability to sleep in (too young for school or homeschooled). The kids can have a snack after school to tide them over.

If this seems too difficult, use some creativity. Maybe breakfast can be eaten together. Or else just really depend on the meals during the weekend to spend quality mealtime together. Even three meals together a week can do wonders and still puts you ahead of national averages.

2. Serving and Cooking the Meal
Preparing the Table

We all know that it is the people and conversation around the table that really attracts and makes us want to come to dinner. This is the lasting beauty that we want. However, a comfortable and attractive dinner table can contribute to this feeling. It can say, "Dinner is a beautiful time together" and "Family members, you are worth this extra time and effort that I put into this meal preparation."

Remember that we all have different situations that will determine what we can do, but we can probably all do something that can improve the physical attractiveness of our dinner table. These suggestions may at first seem as though we need to go out and spend more money. Trust me, I am very thrifty, even stingy at times, so this is not what I am suggesting. If money is tight — and we all need to be wise about what we spend — then we just need to be creative and persistent about attaining these things.

Look for used items. Look for hand-me-downs from parents. Budget for the quality items you want, and shop when there are sales. How about asking for these as Christmas presents? And I am not suggesting that you should go out and get these items right away. Be patient in collecting and purchasing what you need. Use your creativity. This is part of the art of homemaking. Our vocation of wife and mother calls for this.

Here are some things you can consider when setting your table:

Tablecloths or Placemats: I have found both placemats and table-cloths that look great and can also be easily washed. We use placemats for our everyday dinner. They don't always need to be washed, and they can be shaken out, ready to be used again. When they get soiled with food, I simply put just the dirty ones in the washer. I even have a set of vinyl placemats that look like cloth, but can be wiped clean. These are great for messy toddlers and younger children. If this is your crowd, you might want to look for a great set of these. (Save the ABC ones or dino-saur ones for lunchtime — mine have a floral pattern that really adds to the look of my set table.) We use tablecloths on Sundays, holidays, and when guests come over. I don't use tablecloths daily because they require us to do another load of laundry whenever I use them. However, if your table is smaller, it may not add too much to your laundry load. I only use tablecloths that can be safely thrown into the washer, then the drier (or hung outside), and simply folded and put away. No extra soaking or bleaching, and especially no ironing, is needed.

Dishes: Are they stored with easy access? Can the kids get to them so that they can help set the table and put the dishes away? I have a mix of china and plastic everyday dishes for lunch and breakfast, but I also have a different set of matching china plates for dinner. If family restau-rants can use heavy-duty china plates, then so can I. Even the fast-food restaurant Zaxby's uses really nice, brightly colored, heavy china plates for some of their meals. Chicken fingers and french fries are raised to another level when served on nice plates! The first set of dishes I bought were pretty glass dishes from a pottery outlet store. They were 50 cents each. When placed on a lace tablecloth, they actually looked fancy — at least my young family thought so. Now my table has a French country look, with heavier china pieces. Over the course of several years, I've collected matching plates, cups, and serving pieces. Find a look that suits your tastes, home decor, and budget, and see what a little creativity can bring. Do you have fine china collecting dust — or worse yet, boxed up in the attic? I am not suggesting that you let the 18-month-old use a plate, but can this be used better? If the china is too good for your family, then who is it good enough for? Chinaware is meant to be used, not stored. At the least, how about on Sundays and holidays?

Dining Room: I know some families that have a dining room but never use it. They eat in the kitchen, because there is a convenient table there. We do this, too, usually when we are in a hurry, or when dinner is just thrown together. Still, there is something special about sitting down together in the dining room. Dinner in the dining room has a formal feel, and the scene appears to lend itself to a little more lingering and conversation. When we eat in the kitchen, we hurry to get through, and then hurry to get the dishes done. This is fine sometimes, but I think it is better to be the exception and not the rule.

But cleanup is so much easier when eating in the kitchen, right? Well, in most cases it means walking 10 or 20 feet more. Newer, more open, house plans often have the kitchen and dining room together. And some people don't have a dining room at all. I'm just encouraging you to think about what you have, and what is the best way to use it, to make dinner more meaningful for your family. Our home is a traditional house with smaller-sized rooms. One thing that we had to do to accommodate our large family and to make it easy for guests was to change our dining room. We opened the doorway from our kitchen to our former family room so that it is now our dining room. (And yes, we also enclosed a garage to be used as a family room.) Now we are always set up for 12, and can easily add a couple more if need be.

Preparing the Food

Get a Plan — A Menu Is Crucial

The Bible says that *a people without a vision, perish* (see Proverbs 29:18). I say that *a family without a menu plan is famished.* If you really want to do all you can with dinner, you need a menu. Otherwise, like me, you get caught up with the busyness of the week and don't have the time or the energy to prepare good meals. If we do happen to get a wave of inspiration, chances are we'd have to go to the store for missing ingredients or pull a large frozen item out of the freezer and try to defrost it in the microwave. Yes, we've all been there and done that. Most often we settle for the same old standbys or depend on fast food. A menu eliminates all of these problems.

I like to plan a menu weekly, the night before I make a trip to the store. Most of the time I use the grocery store sale fliers for inspiration and economical ideas. Once a week, I try to make something "different." This is probably a recipe I marked in a magazine or pulled off the Internet. I just pull this out and check the ingredients.

(New and exciting meals are literally just a click away. I now subscribe to at least four different menu-planning websites. I'll check them occasionally for new and exciting weekly meal ideas. Having entire menus planned and items listed couldn't be easier with these online meal planners. There is something out there for every taste and budget. We really have no excuse.)

Another thing I do when planning my menu is to do so while looking at my calendar appointments for the week. This way I can see when I need to use the slow cooker, since I'm going to be away all day; or plan for pizza one night, when we are all on our way to a school program; or schedule in when I can have just macaroni and cheese, because my husband and a couple of the older kids are going to the basketball game. I can plan a more involved meal on the day when I have an hour or so before dinner — and something I can whip together when I walk in the door, if we have music practice until 5:00.

Our weekly menu is posted so that everyone can see it.

One more thing to do before finishing the menu is to take a peek in the freezer. I keep meals and meats in one general place in my freezer. I know there are many moms who do the once-a-month cooking deal, but I have tried it and don't really like it. I like the concept of saving some time with preparations, so I use some of those ideas. For example, I will make a double batch of lasagna or chili to serve one that evening for dinner and then freeze the other for another week. I will also brown batches of hamburger to freeze. So many meals can be started with this. Marinating meat in freezer bags — like London Broil in Teriyaki sauce, or chicken breasts in Italian dressing — are great to have in the freezer, even better when they are purchased on sale. These are all conveniently kept in my freezer. (Remember to label. So many times I've thought I wouldn't forget what something was only to have to begin cooking it to figure it out.) So when I am planning my weekly menu, I try to use something from the freezer.

Once I have shopped, I usually tweak and change the menu before posting it on our refrigerator. Sometimes the store may have a great sale on almost-expired chicken that I need to cook that evening, or the store may be out of something else that I have to substitute for. Posting the menu on the refrigerator not only serves to notify everyone of the meals that we are planning to share together, but it also reminds me of what I need to do to get the meal prepped. Do I need to get something out of the freezer? Do I need to allow a lot of time right before the meal, or can I do some cutting and measuring earlier in the day? Do I need to start the meal right when I get up in the morning because it needs to cook in a slow cooker all day? Having the menu posted right where I can't miss it serves as a great visual reminder throughout my busy day.

Another perk to posting the menu on the refrigerator is to remind everyone not to eat the bag of tortilla chips because we are having taco salad in a couple of days. This may be asking too much for some kids to make that connection — but at least it usually works for spouses! I have heard many women complain about their kids getting into the food that was to be used for a meal. Some women put sticky notes on those items that need to be saved — like on the tortilla chips, "Save for Dinner Tues." In our house, if I know that there may be a temptation to use an item that I need for dinner, I simply place it on the really high/hidden shelf in my kitchen, the one with seldom-used appliances and dishes.

This really doesn't happen too often in our kitchen. The food that the kids can prepare to eat is in obvious places, and they generally know what kind of food this is. I always have a basket of fruit, as well as bread with peanut butter and jelly, available. Since four of my children have to pack a lunch daily, I keep a large plastic bin in the pantry of available lunch food. This food can only be eaten if packed. It has such food as granola bars and fruit snacks. If the kids want to add something unusual to their normal food repertoire, they know they need to ask: "Mom, can I have some of this frozen shrimp?" To which I either reply, "No, dear, that is for dinner tonight" or "Sure, dear, I saw it on sale and thought you might like it."

Another idea for meal planning is to use the same basic plan every week: Monday is pasta. Tuesday is chicken. Wednesday is hamburger. Thursday is soup. And Friday is fish. A basic plan like this gives you a good start on your planning, but is open to a lot of flexibility and versatility. I do this partially. We usually have soup on Mondays. And we have a tradition of homemade pizza on Sunday nights.

Following Through on the Plan

Now that everything is planned, preparing is just a matter of carrying it out. When we are tired and worn out prior to dinnertime, it really is a godsend to not have to think, but simply to muster enough energy to go through the motions of preparations. Anyone who has had kids has felt this way. Instead of falling back on fast food or frozen pizza, you know that a warm nutritious dinner is on its way.

Cleanup

After the meal is finished, the tiresome tasks of cleaning up can put a damper on the best of dinners — but it doesn't really have to be that way. In some families, everyone seems to chip in and get the dishes done. I met a woman whose family has the motto: "Mom is the last one to leave the kitchen after dinner," to encourage everyone to stay and get the work done. For us, when everyone has tried to chip in, Mom and Dad invariably seem to do most of the work, occasionally accompanied by a "saintly" kid or two. We solved this problem by assigning simple dinner chores. This way, everyone helps. It also relieves any bitterness or guilt about helping or not helping. And knowing that you have a set chore to do — that the end is in sight — prevents some of the grumbling.

Our Dinner Chore Wheel.

For our chart, we simply have a wheel, made out of two paper plates and a brass fastener, that we spin. We rotate it one place, clockwise at the start of every meal. Currently, we have six chores for our six children who are at home. Keith and I step in to help, or fill in if someone happens to be absent. The tasks are: set the table, clear the table, put the food away, load the dishwasher and wash the pans, wipe the counters and table, and sweep the floor. By not having set chores on set nights, we avoid any unfairness of someone who always "lucks out" and has the "load job" when dinner was eaten out or on the run.

3. The Social and Emotional Atmosphere

Especially for those of us with Martha tendencies, we want to make sure that we can put all the dinnertime stresses, and even the day's stresses, behind and be more like Mary at dinnertime. It is time to sit down and relax at a meal with our family. I know some of you are thinking that dinner with small children is anything but relaxing, but it really is a matter of good preparation and attitude here. Even at a young age, our children can sense when we are feeling stressed — and this, in turn, stresses them out. When we are relaxed and pleasant at meals, our children and husband will more likely be that way, too. This is especially true if they are in the habit of coming to a meal where good food and good laughs will be shared. They will naturally fall into this behavior pattern — most of the time!

Should the kids be made to clean their plates? Should they be made to try the food? These are decisions each family needs to make. I'm not sure there is a right (or wrong) answer. But please keep this general principle in mind: We are trying to create a beautiful and loving atmosphere at dinner for the reasons we listed earlier. We need to choose our battles very wisely.

Personally, we try to encourage the kids to try new foods. We don't make them. Having a new dish every week encourages children to be open to new foods. We also do a lot with different ethnic foods, which makes trying new food fun! We give them a sample size. If they try it and don't like it, then we don't make them finish it. We do, however, insist that the children finish the foods on their plate that they asked for or served themselves. If there is nothing on the table that they like (and we have a couple of really picky eaters), we offer healthy bread and butter as an alternative. I also have a bowl of apples or carrots readily available most of the time. If they refuse to eat their food that they have served themselves, or ate nothing at all for dinner, we will refuse them dessert. For over 20 years and 9 children, we've never had any whining battles at mealtime — and despite not forcing down the vegetables, we've had fairly healthy children who eat a wide variety of foods.

Positive Conversation

Dinner begins and ends with the traditional Catholic mealtime prayers. Sometimes to get the conversation started after everything has been passed around once, my husband asks a question. We used to ask each family member to state their "Good thing for the day," which we adopted from another family we know. Recently, we have been asking the kids: "What did you find interesting today?" Out of that flies many interesting conversational topics.

Our dinnertime conversation is never forced. It flows from the day's events and concerns. When I mention "positive conversation," it means that we never say anything negative about another person, and in general we try to keep the conversation on a positive note. Our conversations usually revolve around an event at school, news from the neighbors, or a movie that we saw. We have debated the best special powers of super heroes, including whether Batman can even be considered a superhero, and which is the best Pokémon.

As the children have gotten into their teens, we have had some political and religious conversations that don't always sound so positive. Should the U.S. attack Iraq? Why does rap music usually have foul language? Why do young women choose to abort their babies? We have kept these issues positive by keeping them from turning into personal insults on other people. In discussing these issues, we have helped to develop our children's critical thinking skills. We also help them to be aware and ready to give a defense of their beliefs without being defensive. The younger ones have learned much from these tough conversations as well. When these serious conversations extend beyond the normal dinnertime, we excuse the younger children or those not interested in the discussion.

Which brings us to two other dinnertime etiquette rules: Children must ask to be excused, and no one leaves until the closing prayer. We use a traditional closing prayer:

> We give Thee thanks, O Lord, for these and all Thy benefits, through Christ our Lord, Amen. May the souls of the faithful departed, through the mercy of God, rest in peace.

MORE MEANINGFUL TIMES

Great conversations, plenty of laughs, and genuine sharing of thoughts and concerns should be the results that we see at our dinnertime. Will this happen all of the time? Of course not. But when it does, it will make all your efforts, and all those other "seemingly" pointless dinners, worth it.

There are other ways to bring meaning to your dinnertime. For example, you could use this time, when all of the family is gathered together, to do family devotions. For some families, this might be every evening. Other families might want to do devotions during particular liturgical seasons such as Advent, Christmas, Lent, or Easter; or on particular days of the week — like Sunday, for instance. We usually do some kind of family devotion during Advent and Lent. In the past, we have used devotionals written for the season; at other times, we've just used the Gospel readings from the Mass of the day. Throughout the year, we celebrate some of the saints' feast days. When we do this, we simply read a short passage about these saints. Often we do this while eating dessert to celebrate the feast day.

I suggest that you don't make these readings too long or boring to tire the kids out. Use discretion as you decide how often and how long to do these activities. We don't want kids to dread coming to dinner. It could defeat all the good that you are trying to do with this activity.

There are many other family activities that might be appropriate for dinnertime. I am particularly aware of ones that deal with the holidays. Since dinners are such an important part of family life, it makes sense that our holidays often revolve around a meal. Here are few things that we do at our holiday meals:

- At Thanksgiving, we go around the table and say what we are thankful for.
- On birthdays, we all say what we like about the birthday person.
- On New Year's Day, we share our resolutions over that peculiar meal of sauerkraut and kielbasa.

Spreading the Joy

One way to especially enrich your dinnertime is to have a very open and welcoming table. And there is no need to wait to have guests at your table until you have "the right dishes" or your family's behavior is "just right." If we waited until everything was perfect, we would never have anyone over for a meal. And let's remember, we especially want to suppress our Martha tendencies here. While simple hospitality is essential on our part, it is the conversation and care that really should matter to our guests. If it isn't, then our guests have the wrong attitude — and it really isn't our problem. Maybe they need a good dose of real "Mary" attention.

Let the kids cook!

Many times, we have a friend right in front of us who could use a good meal and some company. This could be that new neighbor, a new family in church, friends we haven't seen in a while, or friends we just want to spend more time with. I have found that, in my busy schedule, if I don't schedule time for this, I often won't bother. I get so busy and forget all about it. And I have found that when we regularly have people over for dinner, I seem more in tune to looking for others whom I would like to invite.

For our family, we have found that certain times work better for planned dinner invites. For us, we like to use Sunday, after church. We usually have a brunch, which is an easy meal to prepare and serve.

Even though we have planned guests, we should also be open to last-minute invites. When your menu is planned, this is so much easier to do, too. You'll find that your children's friends will often fit this bill. You may think you are doing them a service, providing them with a healthy meal and a little TLC, but actually it is *you* who benefits. Not only does a different voice add some interest to your dinner table, but you will also find out a lot about your kids' friends and their families.

Establishing a good relationship with your children's friends also comes in handy for contact information, rides to places, and an opportunity to influence other kids for the good. You never know what influence you and your family could have on another individual. Just exposing non-Catholic friends (both your friends and your kids' friends) to a positive experience with a Catholic family may influence their decisions about Christianity and Catholicism in the future. You may be planting a seed, along with feeding them.

Remember Mary, and Don't Be "Anxious"

A final note about the emotional and social atmosphere: Just relax. Picture Mary sitting at Christ's feet. That's how we moms should be, despite what is going on around us. And don't picture some idyllic dinnertime in your head and expect your family's dinnertime to look like that. God has given us what He knows we need. Sure, there is always room for improvement. But too often we dwell on what we don't have, instead of loving and enjoying what we do have. Our attitude and mood in the midst of all this will greatly affect the emotional and social atmosphere at the table.

Children are a gift at every stage, and those stages do change quickly. The toddler who always makes a mess also always puts a smile on everyone's face, especially guests.

(On a practical note, when I had so many young ones at my table at one time, I remember someone telling me to expect at every meal that something is going to get spilled. So when it did happen, I expected it, and it wasn't a big deal. No crying over spilt milk. But when it didn't happen, I rejoiced!)

Your Own Solutions

Being like Mary when it comes to mealtimes is very difficult for many of us. We need to sit back and look at ourselves to see how and when we fall into the Martha trap — stressed out and worried about the wrong things.

Sometimes we can sense this right away. I've been so tense when I've been trying to finish up a meal and get everything to the table that I practically bit my husband's head off when he "incorrectly" helped out. Other times, being like Martha is much more subtle. I'll quickly make an excuse for why a child's friend can't stay for dinner because I just don't want to bother preparing any extra food or doing any extra dishes. Sometimes being like Martha is even subtler. I go through the motions of dinner and dishes, cleaning up, etc., and not even one time reflecting or looking for Christ at my dinner table, not even at the mention of His name while saying grace. Becoming more like Mary (one who always looks to Christ) is really the call of every Christian.

iese are hard changes to make in our lives. We need lots of prayer, God's grace to do it. I hope that the "Martha" reflections or practical mealtime suggestions in this chapter, like menu planning, will help make dinner with your family easier for you. Knowing the strengths and weaknesses of your own family will also help you go way beyond my suggestions and enable you to come up with some of your own solutions.

Along the same lines, knowing your own personal strengths and weaknesses (in regards to how you could be more like Mary) should help you look for the changes you need to make as well. Pray and work on these "Mary" changes at your mealtimes in particular, and let these changes spread to the other areas of your life.

✦ ✦ ✦

DINNER RESOURCES

+ *http://www.GraceBeforeMeals.com* (Father Leo's website has cooking videos, recipes, and many tips to help families cook and eat dinner together. You'll love it.)
+ *www.AllRecipes.com* (This is my favorite recipe website. You can search for recipes and ideas by ingredients, topics, etc.)

A few of the many free menu-planning services available in your inbox:

+ *http://www.YouveGotSupper.com*
+ *http://www.RachaelRayMag.com/Recipes/Weekly-Menu-Planner*
+ *www.DineWithoutWhine.com/sample.htm* (This site charges a small fee, but the sample is free.)

A book chockfull of healthy menus:

+ *Saving Dinner: The Menus, Recipes, and Shopping Lists to Bring Your Family Back to the Table*, by Leanne Ely (Ballantine Books, 2003)

Chapter 4

IT'S YOUR HOME, TOO:

Getting the Chores and Work Done
(Hint: "M" Is for Mom, not Maid!)

Many hands make light work. I keep telling myself this over and over again. Whoever said this may not have had in mind that those many hands could be children's hands — and even worse, hands belonging to boys. Having a house of eight boys (and one girl) has certainly been very trying for me. (And as every parent of girls knows, girls can certainly be just as messy!)

Just imagine the first snow day of the year, when all the kids are home from school. They are in and out of the house, all day long, accompanied by friends and neighbors, with many slushy boots, every pair of mittens that can be found, and usually several pairs of wet socks. Not to mention all the coats, hats, scarves, and snow pants. Sure, many hands are in the kitchen, helping to make the hot cocoa, but that's pretty much it.

When it comes to being a Mary in this situation, I am desperately looking for a way to do that without losing my mind. But I know it is there, and I know that I can do it!

After I cheerfully help all the kids make what seems like gallons of hot cocoa, and listen to stories of six-foot snowmen and near-death sledding incidents, I spring into action — not in a yelling or nagging way, but more like a polite drill sergeant. (Of course, everyone came in through the mudroom, so the wet floor is contained on the rug in there.) "Did everyone put his mittens on the mitten-and-hat rack in the mudroom? Are your coats hanging up? Let's put all of those wet clothes into the laundry basket in front of the washing machine." And boots? "If they are not muddy, put them on the boot rack. Otherwise, put them on the back porch."

I'm sure that many of you have similar routines for times like these. And if we didn't have procedures such as these and a place for our winter things, an enjoyable cup of cocoa and conversation with the kids could

The joy of snow!

have been a moment of stress and yelling. That is where our organized, prepared Smart Martha comes in handy.

In this chapter, we will, first of all, examine our common trouble spots and how to deal with them. Second, we will look at ways to eliminate one of the biggest hindrances to keeping a house clean and in order: clutter. And finally, we will consider a way to engage those many hands to help. By putting the suggestions in this chapter to work, you will be surprised to see how fairly clean and orderly your house will become.

TARGET TROUBLE SPOTS, AND "SHARPEN YOUR SAW"

Are wet, rainy days an extra nuisance in your house because of all the mud that gets on your kitchen floor? There are many ways to deal with this. You can get your mop out and mop the floor several times that day. Or you can simply have children remove their shoes before coming in. What about the adults or visitors? Depending on the situation, you can have them remove their shoes, too, or simply use some good doormats, both inside and out. I've read that a properly matted door (two or three steps on both sides of the door) can significantly reduce the amount of dust that comes into your house, besides the debris and mud that immediately come off people's shoes.

Take a cue from public buildings. They are almost always properly matted. And if this method works well for businesses that have to have a clean appearance, yet be time-efficient with cleaning and general maintenance, then you and I can learn something for our busy doors.

Buying mats and putting them at our doors is one example of the precautions we can take to lessen our workload and improve our home's appearance. I call this type of action a *saw-sharpening activity*. The term "saw sharpening" came from a concept in Stephen Covey's book *The 7 Habits of Highly Effective People*, which I describe in the Introduction. But I like this idea so much that it's worth mentioning again. Covey describes a man who has a large pile of wood to cut. This man, however, claims that he is too busy to take time out to sharpen his saw.

This describes us, doesn't it? We are too busy going from one thing to the next. But if this man sawing wood had taken a few minutes away from his work and actually sharpened his saw, his time sawing the rest of the logs would have been significantly reduced.

Now think about mopping that muddy kitchen floor. Instead of having to spend all that time and effort mopping the floor, we could have taken a few extra minutes at a discount store, purchased some mats, laid them down, and over time could have saved substantially more time. But like the man sawing wood, sometimes we just get caught in a rut and don't take the time to do things that will save us substantial time and energy. Often it's just because we have been in the habit of doing things a certain way for so long, and don't realize that we could be doing things better.

This is our first challenge. We need to find our trouble spots by looking for those areas of our homes where we are constantly cleaning or putting items away.

Are there places in your home where things could be arranged differently, making your life a little easier? I am sure many of you have already targeted and solved some of these areas, but I still challenge you to see if there is something else that needs improvement.

As children and family circumstances change, so do our trouble spots. One year, it is dirty diapers staying too long in the garbage can before being taken out — and before you know it, we don't know how to keep soccer uniforms and equipment clean and ready for the next game. It seems as though it was just a minute ago we were tripping over baby toys, and now suddenly we're stumbling over school backpacks. If you are like me, with children of multiple ages, you're struggling with many of these problems simultaneously.

Here is a brief list of some saw-sharpening steps that I have used to make my cleaning routine easier. Your list may be very different than mine. But I hope these ideas will help you think of more ways you can sharpen your own saw:

+ We built a mudroom entrance through our garage, with places to put shoes, coats, etc., when we remodeled our house a few years ago.
+ When we last bought carpeting for inside our home, we installed a beige, speckled berber. Several years later, it still looks great, and

it never looks like it needs to be vacuumed! For great suggestions on carpet colors, look at what is in your doctor's office or the public library.

✦ Fingerprints on walls? Is there a better paint color? Certainly don't use a flat paint, which attracts dirt. In high-traffic areas, we try to use semi-gloss paint, which cleans up so much better than flat paint. Should we be washing hands more?

✦ For countertops, hard floors, and sinks, we found it best to avoid white or dark solid colors. When tiling a bathroom or kitchen, use a darker-colored grout, and use large tiles to limit the amount of grout to scrub.

✦ Bikes all over the yard? We use a fence railing for a bike rack and assign parking spots for all the riding toys.

✦ Pets? We keep the furry ones only in certain rooms. Consider fish. (Just kidding. I'm being too much of a Martha, again.)

✦ Too much mildew in the bathroom? We installed an exhaust fan that automatically comes on with the light.

✦ Furry rugs in the bathroom never in the right place? It wasn't worth it straightening these all of time. We do just fine without them.

Let Your House Do the Housework

These ideas are just the start, but I think you get the idea. And remember, there is a fine balance between utilitarianism and beauty. But with today's choices and a little creativity, I believe we can have both.

Don Aslett wrote a book called *Make Your House Do the Housework*. It is full of ideas for lessening your work around the house. More importantly, the book gets you thinking along these lines. Ask those other Smart Marthas you know for their suggestions, too.

Learn from your past mistakes. We once had beautiful off-white carpeting in our busy family room. It looked lovely — for about a month. We learned our lesson. From then on, all our carpets are brownish/grayish — and after months and years, they still look great. Keeping our house clean (and looking cleaner) in this way epitomizes Smart Martha — we do something "smart" that lessens our time cleaning so that we can be like Mary and spend more time with those we love.

Once you have surveyed your home situation, try out some of your own ideas. I suggest that you keep these thoughts and ideas in your planner/journal, and keep working on them. If the fixes are too costly, work them into your budget or find cheaper alternatives.

This will be an ongoing maintenance project for the rest of your life. Get in the habit now of being on the lookout for these target areas that need some change. Then don't be afraid to *sharpen that saw*. Taking the time to address those problems will save time and energy in the future.

CUTTING CLUTTER

And speaking of sharpening the saw, I should point out that eliminating the clutter in your home is a huge saw-sharpening activity that saves time and helps your house look so much better. If you want the house-cleaning to be done quickly and thoroughly, then get rid of all the extra stuff. Otherwise, the time we spend cleaning is just time spent putting stuff away.

I realize that for some folks, getting rid of extra stuff is extremely stressful. If this is your case, then please ask a friend or relative to help you. Otherwise, just go through the simple steps in this section, and you will unclutter your house.

Have you seen the TLC series *Clean Sweep*? It is about a professional team of organizers who help people clean out a room in their home. You can do the same thing in your home without the professionals. (I know it would be nice to have someone drop by and do it for you, but face it: It's not going to happen!)

We are going to follow the same procedure they do. And it works the same for a whole room, a closet, a bookshelf, or just a drawer.

THE CLEAN SWEEP

Step 1: Empty

This is easy. No need for stress here. Just empty your space. If it's a room with furniture, take everything out but the furniture. For de-cluttering a drawer, it's very easy. Just dump. When my daughter was 15, she had some pretty serious room issues — the main one being that we couldn't see the floor. Her stuff just got out of control. She had too many clothes, too many books, too many I-don't-know-whats. She couldn't be expected to keep her room clean with all that stuff. Most of it had to go. So we started this process.

We got her onboard by telling her that we needed to paint and redecorate her room. What girl wouldn't want that? Yes, you have to take everything out of the room, but it will be worth it. (And at the same time, we helped her to learn how to keep her clutter and stuff to a minimum, as we followed the rest of the steps to put the room back together.)

Step 2: Sort

Again, this doesn't have to be stressful. I had a dreaded drawer in my kitchen that seemed to end up with everything in it. I was putting off cleaning that drawer, but I remembered that I just had to go through the motions of the following steps and it would get done. So I sat down on the kitchen floor, dumped my drawer, and sorted everything into *four piles*:

+ **"Keep Here" pile.** This needs to be carefully thought out, or you'll just end up piling things in here that don't belong. Be very specific. If it is a bedroom, do I want DVDs in here? Do I want this ugly lamp in here? Or if it's a bathroom medicine cabinet, do I want to keep matches in here, or my daily vitamins? Again, be specific.
+ **"Keep, But Not Here" pile.** I had masking tape, a candle, an extension cord, a dozen extra pens, and a hot pad in this pile from my drawer.
+ **"Give Away" pile.** When we did my daughter's room, this pile was huge. We just kept filling up garbage bags of items to donate. When these bags were full, we tied them shut and took them right to the car. Granted, this step can be very stressful. If we are working with someone who is a little hesitant about getting rid of her stuff (even if it's yourself), you can put the stuff into storage, like your attic or garage, for (fill in the blank) months. (Make whatever "deal" you have to make to get it done.) When that time is up, and you haven't needed anything in those bags, then take them straight to a charity. (Don't sneak a peek into those bags. Just send them on their way!)
+ **"Throw Away" pile.** From my kitchen drawer, I had some broken pencils, a popsicle stick, and some old candy. No "keepers" there.

Step 3: Put It Away

This is probably the hardest step. Get rid of the "Give Away" bag/pile. Next, you need to get rid of the "Throw Away" bag/pile. With the "Keep, But Not Here" pile, begin by sorting this into piles according to the rooms the stuff belongs in. Break it all down into smaller piles, if needed. All the while keep asking yourself, "Do I really need this?" I have a saying that I always tell the ladies at my seminars: "A place for everything *wanted*, and everything *wanted* in its place."

Don't keep things if you don't use them or "want" them, and don't just keep things because you have places for them. What good is a perfectly organized shelf of stuff, all labeled and in bins, if the stuff is not actually used? So, after you've given these items a second look, and divided them into easier piles to put away, just deliver your piles accordingly. This is where kids can be very helpful. Give each kid a different pile to put away.

The last pile to deal with is the "Keep Here" pile. You've determined the purpose for this space and what belongs here. Now you have to decide how to best store the items in this space. Keep in mind that you'll want easiest access to the things you use most often. Stuff that is not used as often can be tucked away, but still make sure you can access it.

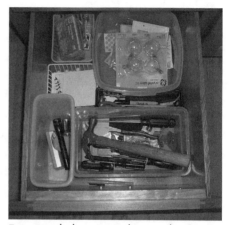

During the process, ask yourself if you need better storage containers. Research your options. For my drawer in the kitchen, I came up with six categories of objects I wanted to keep in that

Even a junk drawer can have order.

drawer: (1) matches, (2) pens and memo pads, (3) flashlights, (4) tools, (5) light bulbs, and (6) dry-erase markers.

Next, I found properly-sized storage baskets or bins to hold each category of items. I didn't find the perfect container for the matches, so I temporarily put them in a Tupperware container and made a note on my grocery list to find this bin on my next trip to store. I made use of a Tupperware container for the flashlights, another container for the light bulbs, a small plastic basket for the pens and pads, and a plastic shoebox-sized bin for my tools.

Step 4: Share the Vision

This, too, can be a difficult step — but if it is forgotten or set aside, then chances are you will be cleaning this drawer/room/closet/shelf again very soon. To "share the vision," simply tell everyone about the space you have cleaned up and where the things from this space now are.

(Obviously, if it is your underwear drawer, please keep this to yourself.) But for my kitchen "junk" drawer, I simply announced: "Hey, everyone, look! This drawer is for these six types of things, and they are put in these six different containers. Thanks!" They may not remember next week when they are looking for a screwdriver, but inevitably they will open the drawer, sort of recall something that Mom said, and most likely put it back in the bin where it belongs.

This is not 100 percent guaranteed, but I think we stand a better chance when we can "share the vision" with the rest of the family. If the organization plan is not obvious to your kids and spouse, try using labels. I've been known to write on the shelf with a pencil or marker, write on the bin, print out computer labels, draw pictures, use a photo, and so on. Anything to make the *vision* I have for this space easier to preserve.

If I were going to write another step, I'd probably say: "Step 5: Start Over." Many times, however, if you've done a clean sweep of an area, you may just need to do a quick tidying up or a partial "clean sweep." For example, my clothes closet always looks a mess. And usually, it's not that it needs to be completely cleaned out, but rather it just needs to be tidied up. Someone — that's me — hasn't been *sharing the vision* of where things belong and has been piling things up.

✦ ✦ ✦

Does your whole house need a clean sweep? Don't despair! As I heard one woman at my seminar say: Be thankful you have a house filled with possessions. Many people in the world are homeless or are refugees. Considering this may help you quit feeling sorry for yourself. But you still need to take the plunge and do something to get yourself out from under this clutter mess.

For someone who may find herself knee- or waist-deep in clutter, I suggest that you get some help. Beg friends, pay professionals, or use family. Do whatever it takes. Don't be too proud.

Next, come up with a plan. Do one room every weekend, for example.

Finally, just dig in and start to work. Be steady and persistent. You'll be surprised at the progress you make. *You can be clutter-free!*

One of my lists in my journal/planner is a de-clutter list. I simply list all of the areas in my home where I need to do this process. If you are starting this process for your entire home, your list may contain larger areas like entire rooms or closets. For me, at this point, my jobs are smaller and very specific, such as "the second shelf in the downstairs bathroom cabinet" or "the top-left desk drawer." I try to do one of these a week.

I am always adding to this list — the medicine cabinet, the spice rack, my jewelry drawer, and on and on. And yes, I sometimes still have to throw in an entire room.

OTHER CLUTTER BUSTERS

If things tend to always pile up in your home, you need to determine why this is so. It may be clutter. It may be that these things don't have a place.

Do your kids constantly have their clean clothes out of their dresser drawers? Is this because their drawers are overstuffed? Or does someone lack the discipline to keep those things put away (as in the case of my closet)? Here is where you must determine if you need to clean sweep a spot or come up with a solution for a particular area of clutter. Remember, you can't really start to clean until everything is put away.

Trust me: If you put your mind to it, you can solve your clutter problems.

Helping Kids Control Their Clutter

How about the problem of kids just simply leaving their things about? I imagine that every home with kids has this problem. Don't despair if you feel like you spend too much time picking up their stuff. Here's a solution I tried a few times. It didn't work great for me, but I will pass it on to you because I've heard that other moms have had success with it. And actually, just starting this effort does wake your children up to your mission.

First, announce to everyone that WE are going to start to control our clutter better, and that WE are going to try it for two weeks. During this time, if anyone leaves anything out, you simply collect it in a large box. At the end of the day, the children have to pay a small amount to get their items back.

What if they don't care about getting the item back? I make them pay anyway, because somebody else had to clean it up for them. What if someone else used the item and left it out? Whoever had it out has to pay. (Honestly, I found this to be a little too complicated and time-consuming for me. But as I already said, this effort does illustrate the problem to everyone, so it may be worth your time. You may even earn some cash!)

What I now do instead, when I find someone's item left out and he isn't a soft-yelling distance away, is put the item on his "stair" (or laundry bin, if a younger child), whichever I am closer to. (My teens don't have laundry bins downstairs, so all of their stuff goes on their "stair.") Each child has a "stair" on the staircase that leads up to the bedrooms. Gabriel's is the first one. Jacob's is the second. Joseph's is the third, etc. My daughter used to have the "stair basket" on her stair because she always left the most stuff lying around.

Since these stairs are at our front entrance, I try to make sure the stairs get cleared daily. Instead of me telling each child to put his stuff on his stair away, I simply make this someone's daily chore. The person with the "stair" chore must carry the stuff on each stair upstairs and place it on this or that person's bed, or he can request the person to do it himself, especially if it is a lot of stuff. For the younger children, their stuff in their laundry bin goes away when they have to put their laundry away. This is done weekly or more frequently, whenever their bin gets full.

Daily Clutter Busters: "Rules to Live By"

1. **Leave a room better than when you found it.** When you leave a room, pick up something that goes somewhere else and get it closer to its destination; or put something away; or throw something away; or even just straighten a pillow or a picture.

2. **Get those dirty clothes into the basket.** Getting them up and in the basket, not on the dresser, or on the floor, or on a chair keeps this little bit of clutter under control.

3. **Take care of your mail and daily paper.** Don't let these pile up. Sort your mail daily. Have a place for your daily paper. When I retrieve the new one, the old one goes into the recycle bin.

4. **Take out your trash.** This is the potentially smelly stuff in the kitchen. If your bag isn't quite full, get stuff from other trash cans and fill it.

5. **Before bed, do a five-minute tidy.** I'm always amazed at what a simple five-minute cleanup can accomplish. You will feel refreshed in the morning to wake up to a "clean" house.

6. **Something in, something out.** Another important point, especially once you have your clutter and piles under control, is: **When something comes in, something must go out.** This is why I always have a tall laundry basket lined with a garbage bag easily accessible in my closet. This is my "Give to Goodwill" bag. When it gets full, I simply pull it out, stick it in my trunk, and drop it off on my next trip.

This plan has done the trick for us. For the most part, I have recognized where the clutter and piles begin and have circumvented these. It seems that many busy families have piles of stuff near their entryway. Cubbies or other neat "dumping" spots can be stationed here. I still have trouble with backpacks, because the kids like to bring them farther into the house, past the entryway, but not quite up to their desks. Good old-fashioned nagging was my final solution for this: "Either put them on your hook in the mudroom or take them up to your desk in your bedroom!"

Our giveaway basket is in my closet.

Now that we have everything picked up — or at least have a place for everything wanted — it's time to clean!

COME UP WITH YOUR FAMILY'S OWN CLEANING PLAN

Have you ever tried to follow a cleaning plan that you got off the Internet or read in a book? I have. Countless times. And I can say that, if you are like most women, it may work for a while, but then you quit. Sure, we may learn some things, and we may pick up some good habits. But for a cleaning plan to work, it has to be yours.

In the first place, each family has a different level of tolerance when it comes to cleanliness. What one person considers clean, another might feel is untidy. Have you ever experienced this? As I mentioned earlier, I have walked into homes that I felt were very clean by my standards, only to have the mother apologize for such a "messy" home. I have tried this when these moms have come over to my house, but this has been when my home was considered clean. Notice, I just "apologize" for the mess; I resist the temptation to say, "It's usually much cleaner." (I could add, as a plaque in my mother's kitchen put it: "My house doesn't always look like this. Sometimes it is even worse.")

Related to this are the differences in personalities within the family. Sandra Felton has written many books to help "Messies" keep their houses clean. She relates how people generally fall into two categories:

"Messies" and "Cleanies." Do you live with a lot of Messies? or Cleanies? or both?

And besides having different levels of cleanliness, both in making messes and in what we consider clean, we also have many other differences, such as the number of children, their ages, and their personalities. If you are raising toddlers, for instance, your messes and your helpers will be very different than those of a house with teens. I am not saying which one is worse! Then, added to that, there are some families that have the means to hire a maid and have larger spaces, which may or may not mean more work.

Because of all of these differences, each family needs to come up with a cleaning plan that will work for them.

DETERMINE WHAT NEEDS TO BE DONE FOR YOUR HOUSE TO BE CONSIDERED "CLEAN"

This may seem like an obvious step, but have you ever sat down and written these actions out? *I am challenging you to do this now.* There is a chart at the end of this chapter, on page 113. Don't be afraid to use it. You might have to find a sharpened pencil, though. (Yes, I have one in my kitchen drawer. Please put it back in the basket there when you're done.)

Your Daily "To Do's" — A Good Foundation

Many of the daily things on your list will be things that you will need to do yourself. This is to be expected. To really keep your home in "clean mode," you will need to be very disciplined about keeping your own daily "to do's" done. It will be a matter of discipline for a while, but eventually it becomes a habit, like making your bed. If you don't make your bed immediately when you get up.... This is a good one to put at the top of your list.

My other dailies are:

+ Do two loads of laundry.
+ Pick up all of my own clothes.
+ Do a five-minute cleanup in the bathroom, which includes spraying the shower with a daily cleaner, every other day.
+ Keep the kitchen clean — dishes done, counters wiped and cleared.
+ Make dinner.

✦ Check up on my other "to do's" or "BOCs" (see below).

✦ See if the children's chores are getting done.

Add to this your daily "Clutter Busters" and you really will see a big difference in how clean your home appears.

Over all, when you list your chores like this, it does seem like a lot of work. But when it becomes part of your daily routine, as simple as taking a few minutes here and there, it really doesn't take very long. This is especially true if you don't take a lot of time to think about it or complain about it — and just do it. I do many more cleaning tasks than this on a good day; and on a bad day, I barely get through all of it. I find, though, that being disciplined about my dailies makes a world of difference in my house feeling clean and all together.

Think about what would help in your situation if certain things were done every day. But don't get too carried away with your list. Keep it simple. Then get it done. Speedy and steady will help you win this race.

BOC (Big and Occasional Chores)

In my experience, the simpler the plan, the better. You don't need to decide right now what needs to be done every fifth Tuesday or even once a year. We are just going to start with the basic daily and weekly things. After this is going well, and if you are the kind of person who likes details and lists, you should add the monthly, seasonal, and yearly chores. I have found, though, that for most women (well over 51 percent?), if we can manage these daily and weekly chores, we can take care of the others on a need-to-do basis.

For example, as I am doing my weekly dusting in the living room, I realize that I haven't washed the curtains in there for a long time. Immediately, I get a pencil and write this down in my planner. (If I had time, I would take them down and put them in the washer at that moment.) This is your giant to-do list. I call it my BOC: "Big and Occasional Chores." I regularly turn to this list and hammer away at it. Surprisingly, these things get done. I will reveal how in a few paragraphs.

When you start to look for these things, you will find them. If not, hopefully no one else will. Again, if this seems too spontaneous for you, put "wash curtains in living room" into your seasonal to-do list. Either way, do what works for you. (I even keep a crossed-off list. Occasionally, I will look back through it and see if there is something that needs to be done again that perhaps I've overlooked.)

The Daily and Weekly Chores

For the situation in our current home, we have the following tasks as our daily and monthly tasks. (Our dinner chores are separate.) Notice that *my* daily to-dos are listed here as well:

+ **Daily:** Clean all bathrooms, except the showers/tubs. Tidy up all rooms, carport, and porches. Clear the stairs. Take out the trash. Take care of the animals. Take out the compost.
+ **Weekly:** Clean windows in kitchen. Clean showers/tubs. Vacuum all carpeting and stairs. Dust. Mop kitchen. Sweep porches. Blow off and clean back patio. Take up bins of clothes from laundry room and put away or do your own laundry. Tidy up the yard.

Your cleaning plan will be different from ours. When attempting a list for the first time, you may have to change it, moving things from weekly to daily, daily to weekly, and finding other tasks to add to these lists. Once you have good lists, the next step is to assign these jobs.

ASSIGNING CHORES: "IT'S YOUR HOUSE, TOO"

When it comes to assigning chores, the prevalent opinion among children today is: "No one else has to do chores." And although I have to admit that I'm sure there are some children who don't do chores, I know for a fact that there are many children who really do chores. I always have the usual names that I spill out to my kids when they have such complaints — my children's friends, with whose mothers I have discussed such matters.

But I have even more definitive proof for you. This book! If it's in writing, it must be true. Here is a family with kids, of all ages, who do chores. And just think of the millions of children who are also now doing chores, whose mothers have read the same book!

I always impress on my children that, first of all, I am not their maid, nor their waitress. Sure, it's my "job" to keep the house clean, but it's their job, too. They live here. They enjoy the benefits of living here. They should also share in the work. I think that goes for spouses as well. After all, we are a family that shares life together, including the upkeep of the house.

With this in mind, we simply need to divvy up all these tasks that have to be done. I make it very simple. (Simple always works best. The simpler the plan, the more likely we will stick to it.)

I like giving each child his daily chores and his weekly chores. I pretty much do all of the other chores, with my husband chipping in, although he usually has his own Dad's List that he works on. The kids are responsible for doing their daily chores every day. Ideally, I should check to see if they have completed their chores every day. This is probably what you should do.

But I must confess that I'm not that consistent. What I do instead is remind the kids to do their daily chores when I see they have time or when I notice a chore not done. I know this seems sporadic. But to add consistency to my method, I muster up enough energy to check on those daily chores twice a week. (To see how I divide up the chores among the children we now have at home, please see the chart at the end of this chapter, on page 115.)

Shares of the "Kiser Wealth"

If the children have done their daily chores on the two "checked" chore days, they are rewarded with a share of the "Kiser wealth." (Our extra chore day is Saturday, when they are required to do their weekly chores.) If their daily chores or weekly chores are not done, they will incur a fine. Usually, the fine is for the same amount they receive for one of their checked chore days. Some people call this kind of sharing "allowances."

We don't like to use the term "allowances." Nor do we like to refer to the kids getting "paid" for doing their chores. After all, this is their house, too. My husband and I are not their employers or their maids. We all chip in to get our house taken care of — and because of that, we all share in part of the Kiser wealth, according to age and need.

If you are not doing your share, you don't get your share. We all get shelter, food, clothing, education, entertainment, and a little spending money. As the children get older, they can take over some of these needs for themselves, and thus receive a larger portion of the Kiser wealth. My husband and I also believe that as the children get old enough to get a job, they can contribute to their own needs, particularly entertainment. In other words, as our kids enter high school, we raise their "allowances," and we expect them to get some kind of job over the summer. This extra money covers those extra expenses that teens incur.

Where Keith and I draw the line on what we buy for them, and what they buy for themselves, follows a few simple rules:

+ We buy them the clothing and shoes that we feel are "necessary." Often these are secondhand clothes that we receive as hand-me-downs or that I purchase at Goodwill or consignment shops. If these are not "good enough" for the kids, they are free to buy their own clothes with their own money, although very few of our children do this.

+ We also have a general rule that we pay $30-$40 toward tennis shoes. I can usually find a pair on sale for this amount. If you have teens, you probably know that the "on sale" ones aren't always preferred. If this is the case, then they just add their own money to get the pair they really want. This same idea applies for other necessary items that aren't easily available secondhand.

+ Another rule we follow for the kids of all ages is that we pay for half of the birthday presents they have to buy for birthday parties.

+ For the teens, we pay for half of any camp, retreat, or optional field trip they want to attend. This helps them decide how badly they want to participate. If they have to save up half of the money to go on a trip to Spain or soccer camp, you better believe that they will try to get the most out of it.

+ Finally, for the teens, most of their entertainment needs are purchased from their own stash. This includes fast food, music, movies, dates, and dances.

Learning to budget, save, and spend money is an invaluable lesson that kids need to learn before they are on their own. This is a very simple way that we have managed to do this. The more your children do this under your supervision, the better. From the experience of having three kids away at college now, I am certain that these college students know how to spot a bargain and to purchase only items on sale, with the awareness that fashionable, name-brand clothes cost only a few dollars at the thrift store.

DOING THE WEEKLY AND BOC

It's your decision when to do the weekly chores and the BOC (Big and Occasional Chores) that I mentioned earlier. We usually do the weekly and some BOC on Saturday morning. If there are soccer games, baseball games, or basketball games on Saturday (and we've had all of these), then we either work the chores before, after, or on another day. If we have to miss weekly chores occasionally, we just make up for it on the next free Saturday. The house won't fall in.

It is really amazing to me how much work gets done if everyone, including Dad, jumps in and works for just one hour. Your weekly chores, plus some extras, will get done. We don't offer pay for this. Our rule is simply that no one leaves the house until his chores/our chores are done. In our home, Keith and I will sometimes work a little longer with a kid or two to finish off those larger chores or house projects.

LEARNING THEIR CHORES WELL

Making sure each child knows how to do his chore is worth every minute you take to do this. This is one reason that we rotate chores infrequently, so every kid can learn do his chore very well. Another reason is because it is simpler for me to remember whose chore is whose. If I walk into a really messy bathroom, I know immediately whose job it was, and I tell him to get to it. I don't have to go into another room, pull out a chart, and know the date in order to figure out who was supposed to clean that bathroom. The kids really get good at doing their chores from repetition. Finally, by having the kids keep the same chore for months at a time, we don't have to deal with the claim of injustice in having to switch chores with someone "even when he didn't get it done and now I have a bigger mess to clean up!"

For some chores, you may need to specifically write out a checklist of steps to show what needs to be done. Encourage the kids to read through this list every time they do the chore, until they've got it down.

Although I haven't given any specifics on how to do any particular chore in this book, I do have a cleaning video that I share at my seminar. It goes through the steps you follow to clean any bathroom — and it's narrated and demonstrated by a 10-year-old boy! Instructions on how to order one are on my webpage: *www.SmartMartha.com*.

Chores for Little Ones

I know that some of you have a house full of mess makers (those adorable toddlers) and not so many mess cleaners. You are probably dreaming of the day when you can sit around while your older children slave away, cleaning the house. I, too, used to have such visions. I actually had five children under the age of 5 once. And although it is easier once you have some children able to help out more, somehow our workload seems also to multiply as they age.

When my children were just at the age when they could start doing chores, I used a pocket-card system. Every day, each child needed to complete the chores on the cards in their pocket. The cards were just index cards with pictures drawn on them to represent the chore. (You could use a photograph.) One card had a bed on it for making their beds. Another card had a toy bin, which meant "Pick up the toys." Another had a plate and silverware, which meant "Set the table."

Pocket charts can hold index cards with chores listed on them.

Each child had a little paper pocket — in their color, with their name on it — stuck on the refrigerator. The pockets were made out of construction paper about the size of a greeting card. When the chore was done, they took the card out and put it in another pocket labeled "Done."

This is a very easy and flexible system that can actually be used for children of all ages. It's very easy to rotate chores with this system. Instead of pictures on the index cards, chores with the steps written out on them could be used for more detailed chores for older kids.

Age-Appropriate Chores

It's up to individual parents to decide when children should start doing chores, and what they are capable of doing. It seems like a long time before children actually begin to make contributions toward keeping the house clean, but we know that doing chores adds to their sense of belonging and establishes good habits. I think that by age 3 or 4, they can certainly help by picking up toys, setting the table, cleaning mirrors or windows or walls at their height, and making their bed. By age 5 or 6, they can put away the silverware from the dishwasher, keep their rooms clean, empty trash cans, dust, and even vacuum. My 5-year-old loves to mop!

Now, I didn't say they could do these things well, but they can at least contribute somewhat. And, of course, every child is unique — some 4-year-olds can clean a bedroom better than some 11-year-olds. When they are young like this — under 7 — chores should still be somewhat fun! They will get a real sense of being a "big girl" or "big boy" by helping Mommy. If not, lay off for a while or, at the least, use a reward system, not punishments.

Chores for Older Teens

As our children have entered the later teen years, they have become less and less available to work at home. Often this is attributed to schoolwork, sports, music lessons, plays, and outside employment. Our older teens hardly have anytime to spend at home. The last thing I want to do is to use those precious minutes in those last years at home to nag them about their chores. We have learned to be flexible about this and go with the seasons (soccer season, play season, etc.).

Another helpful tip that I learned from a Smart Martha at one of my seminars was to offer cash to the other children for the chores that the teenagers were not able to do. This cash came from the share that was part of the teen's "allowance." This mom put the chore money for the chores that weren't completed on the table every Sunday at 6:00. Whoever wanted to finish those chores got the money.

I adapted this for our family. On the day following my checked paydays (Monday and Thursday), I offer part of the teen's chore money to do the chores that he was too busy to do. My anxious preteens, often the best workers, look forward to this opportunity. Everyone is happy. The older teens don't get into trouble or nagged for not doing their work, the younger teens or preteens get more money because they did the chores, and Mom is happy because the house gets cleaned.

How do I keep track of all the money? I have tried to do it with cash, but that was impossible for me. I now have a chart on the side of my refrigerator. (Look at my sample at the end of this chapter, on page 115.) On the checked chore days (Monday and Thursday), I write down the date and the money I owe them. If they need money, they can take a withdrawal. I simply write the withdrawal amount with the date and the reason (if applicable) so that they remember where their money went. By writing these things down and keeping track of the money where everyone can see, I never have to worry about who owes whom.

LAUNDRY

Do clothes really multiply in the laundry room? Do socks get eaten in the dryer? Why do I find myself washing clean clothes, including some that even have their crease lines? Can 14-year-olds do their own laundry? Out of all these, the only question I will attempt to answer here is the last — and the answer is yes! I will let you ponder the rest when you have time to meditate on these and the other mysteries of life.

Some families like to have one day dedicated to laundry. Me? I like to do one or two loads a day.

When I first get up in the morning, I get the laundry started. Throughout the rest of the morning, I make a couple more stops in the laundry room, and usually that's all it takes. We all like to complain about the laundry — but for pity's sake, it's not like we have to haul it down to the river and pound it on rocks. Honestly, for me, if I follow my laundry system, which includes doing one or two loads a day, I hardly ever have any laundry woes.

CUTTING DOWN ON LAUNDRY

1. Teens Can Do Their Own

Before I share my laundry system, I want to share some tips that may help reduce the amount of dirty clothes that you have to wash. The most productive one is to have your high schoolers wash their own clothes. I know I mentioned before that they seem too busy for many other chores. Doing their own laundry is a great way for teens to contribute to the household. What is best about this is that it is practically self-checking. You really don't have to nag them about getting their laundry done. If their laundry isn't done, they simply don't have the (clean) clothes they want to wear.

(And yes, I have had that teenager who didn't care if he wore dirty clothes. He took a little more prodding. But for the most part, if he didn't care, neither did I. I did insist on clean clothes for church, however.)

This motivation works for most teenagers. Plus, *when* they do their laundry is completely up to them. Let's face it. Teens like this independence. It also gets them ready for when they have to do their laundry in college.

For my teen boys, they each have their own laundry basket in their room. When this is filled with dirty clothes, they bring it down and wash it. One basket is about one load. For my daughter, I've encouraged her to use two baskets so that she can separate her lights from her darks. When one of these gets full, she brings it down and washes it in the right temperature. My teens like doing their own laundry because this way their clothes never wind up with the wrong person. (I know you won't believe this, but I have inadvertently given clothes to the wrong child!)

2. Don't Have Too Many Towels

Do you find yourself washing towels all the time? I've solved this problem in my house by assigning every child a specific towel and a specific place to hang the towel. We have towel assignment by color. This way, no one uses your towel. If you forget to hang your towel up when you get out of the shower, you will have a wet, smelly towel the next time you get out of the shower. I even went so far as to hide all the extra towels in our house. My kids learned to be responsible with their towels. In summer, I do a similar thing with the beach towels. They go right onto the clothesline when they come back from the pool.

How long do towels last between washes this way? I usually go about two weeks. I mean, you are clean when you get out of the tub, so only clean water goes onto the towel and then the towel hangs to dry. The teenagers who are doing their own laundry actually wash their towels more frequently because they wash them when they wash their clothes. (It might also be because they are more likely to forget to hang up their towel, and then notice that it gets smelly.)

Having places to hang the towels is sometimes harder if many children share a bathroom. Drying racks that can hang on the wall work well. When we had a home with only two bathrooms, we used hooks on the back of the kids' doors for their towels. They seemed to work to dry the towels adequately. We also had towels made with hoods on them. Not only were these great for toddlers to wrap themselves up in when they got out of the tub, but they were then easy to hang onto a hook.

3. Recycle

If we can get our kids to wear some of their clothes more than once, this could also greatly reduce our laundry. I like to encourage my kids to wear their jeans or athletic pants more than once. If they can be worn again, I tell them to hang the pants on a hook in their closet. Some kids get carried away and wear them for several days. But, hey, that means you have that much less laundry to do — and let's also not forget how "green" we are by doing this! I also encourage them to wear their sweatshirts and hoodies more than once.

4. Keep Order

Finally, just by keeping the laundry neat, orderly, and caught up, we are less likely to find ourselves washing clothes that are still clean.

WHAT A LAUNDRY ROOM SHOULD HAVE

I have a very simple laundry system. Perhaps I'll start by telling you what I think every laundry room needs:

1. Bins or suitable places for everyone's clothes that are washed. For me, I use plastic bins that are stackable drawers that slide out. Dish bins on a shelf or a table serve the same purpose. Having mine stacked saves me a lot of room. When a person's bin is full, he carries it to his room, puts the clothes away, and brings down the empty bin.
2. Laundry baskets for sorting dirty clothes. I have three: one each for whites, darks, and lights.
3. A bin or place for washed dishtowels/kitchen towels.
4. A bin or place for washed rags or cleaning clothes.
5. A place for extra hangers — at least 10. I encourage everyone, when an item is taken off a hanger from his or her closet, to put the empty hanger into the dirty-clothes basket. That way, all the hangers end up in the laundry room, where they are needed.
6. A place to hang the clothes right out of the dryer. I have a hanging clothes bar above all my bins. It is divided into sections for each person. This way I am only sorting the hanging clothes once.
7. A radio or CD player. Think about it. You could listen to the news, books on tape, or learn a whole other language while you are in there.
8. A rack to hang lingerie or other clothing that needs to be hung up to dry.
9. A catch-all basket for the goodies you find in the washer and dryer, or take out of people's pants. (Sorting all of this stuff and putting it away is a good job for someone in trouble.)
10. Shelf, basket, or something to hold your laundry detergent and stain removers.
11. Wastebasket for the lint and other trash you find.
12. A bin or basket for paired socks.
13. A bin or basket for single socks.
14. Optional: A sewing kit for those small repairs.
15. Optional: I have a laundry sink with a soak bucket ready to soak heavy-duty stains or to wash hand-washables.

I know this may seem like a lot of stuff to have in a laundry room, but remember that many of these bins are stacked like a stack of drawers.

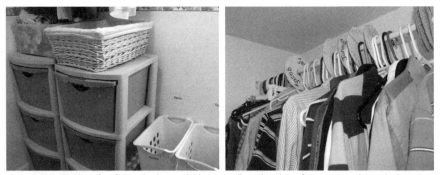

These are my bins for folded, clean clothes, and my baskets for sorting dirty clothes.
Above my bins and sorting baskets, I have a bar for hanging clothes.

I also have shelves, and I use every bit of wall space. And for folks that don't have a laundry room, you still need these things; you'll just have to be a little more creative on what you use and where you put them. You'll have to use shelves, racks, and temporary bins, counters, cupboards, etc.

Another suggestion for those without a laundry room is to do laundry once or twice week — treat it like a weekly chore that you do every Tuesday night, for example. You just need to find a good way to stash all of the dirty clothes — perhaps just in larger hampers.

A SIMPLE LAUNDRY SYSTEM

Once you get your laundry room in order, a simple laundry system is all you need. We have a laundry basket/hamper in each bedroom for the dirty clothes. Some families put one in the bathroom. When this basket gets full, somebody is assigned to bring it down. Whoever brings it down sorts it into the three sorting laundry baskets (whites, darks, lights) in the laundry room. For my daily loads, I usually start with the fullest sorting basket and wash it. If a basket isn't full, I usually go find a full hamper from someone's room and sort it.

As soon as the dryer goes off, I get the clothes that go on hangers out of the dryer and hang them up on my hanging bar in their correct, labeled spot. Doing this practically eliminates any need for ironing. In this day and age, with many non-ironing fabrics, I believe that ironing is almost obsolete. And, of course, if I'm not there when the dryer goes off, I'll tumble them in the dryer again for 10 minutes. (I probably do this more than I should — so much for being "green.") If the load is sheets or comforters, I do use my clothesline. One of these days, I hope to use my clothesline for more of my laundry.

When I am folding clothes, I put them directly into that particular child's bin. Each bin is labeled and kept in the same spot. When a bin gets full, the bin's "owner" has to put his clothes away. The kitchen towels get put away when its bin is full, and the rags/cleaning cloths just stay in the laundry room for people to get when needed.

Socks are a stinky subject for me. I am so happy for summer, when the kids usually just wear flip-flops or are barefooted.

I've never tried having the children clip or pin their socks together in pairs before putting them into the dirty clothes. This would be asking for failure. I have enough trouble getting the clothes into the dirty-clothes baskets, period. (And on this note, I have found that hampers or clothes-baskets without lids, although not as neat looking, stand a better chance of attracting the dirty clothes than those with lids.)

Regarding socks, I just hope that most pairs end up in the same load. If I come up with a stray sock, it goes in a basket I have placed between the washer and dryer. I usually rest them on the sides of the basket in hopes that its pair will show up soon.

I keep all of the pairs of socks I find in a "paired-sock basket." Instead of sorting the paired socks into our own individual bins — since it is very difficult to tell whose socks are whose — I just put them all in this basket. (I make an exception for my own and my husband's socks, since these are easily recognizable. They go right into our bins.) When the children need socks, they just get them out of the paired-sock basket in the laundry room.

About once a month, someone has the tedious job of pairing the stray socks. (I'm not sure how I get so many — thus, the sore subject.) I often do it myself while watching a movie. Another tip to pairing socks: I have found that it works best with the no-show and ankle socks to pair them by putting one of the socks completely inside its pair. This way, when children are looking for the socks that are their size, they don't have to pull pairs apart in the process. A paired-sock basket wouldn't work with a laundry room in a basement, but a stray-sock basket would still work.

Ideally, if I were building a home, I would stick to ground-floor laundry, as I have now. It's so convenient to do my two loads right where I spend most of the day. Muddy or dirty clothes from outside can come right into the laundry room. What's the one thing I would change? I would love to have a chute from an upstairs hallway. This would save all of the time carrying down the dirty-clothes baskets and keep so much of the dirty-clothes mess out of the children's rooms.

Sometimes we have clothes that we aren't really sure where to put them. An example of this is clothes that need to be repaired. I keep all of the sewing repairs I need to do in a large wicker basket next to my sewing machine, which is in my bedroom. Ideally, I would do the repairs the minute I see them, but sometimes it's just as easy to let them pile up and tackle them all while I have the equipment up and running. Usually, these items to be sewn and repaired show up in the wash. Because my sewing machine is in my bedroom, I just wash the items needing to be repaired and put them in my clean-clothes bin. When I put my clothes away in my bin, the clothes that are to be repaired simply go into the sewing-repairs wicker basket in my bedroom.

✦ ✦ ✦

And there you have it. Is there something that you could adapt from my laundry system to help yours? Think about where your problems are and what you can do to fix them. Take the time to "sharpen your saw" here so that you can save a little time on your laundry.

—— HELP! SOMEONE HAS RANSACKED MY HOUSE! ——
(How to Clean a Really Messy Toy Room)

Maybe this hasn't happened to you — and actually, it hasn't really happened to me — but I've seen a toy room/game room look as though a thief had dumped all of the toys out in a futile effort to find some treasure hidden in one of the bins. Maybe you've had a really busy couple of weeks. Maybe you've been sick or away. Maybe you've been watching your friend's children. Or maybe the neighborhood has been hanging out at your house!

Whatever the case, somehow you've got a huge mess in your toy room/bedroom/game room/basement/you-name-it. Despite all your efforts at de-cluttering the toys, using child locks, and trying to consistently keep the toys put away, *everything* — toys, games, puzzles — is out on the floor.

MAKE IT A GAME

Don't despair. There are ways to deal with this in a Mary-like manner, even though you may feel as Jesus did when He had to clear the Temple of vendors. Here is a list of game-like strategies that you can use to motivate your kids to clean up the mess:

+ **"The Timer"**: Sometimes simply setting a timer is enough motivation to get kids moving to pick up.
+ **"Trapped!"**: Another easy method is to trap all of the kids (sometimes with the parents, too) in the messy room with no means of escape until the room is clean.
+ **"4 Square" (or "3 Square" or "2 Square" or "6 Square")**: I get a piece of chalk and divide the room into as many squares as I have cleaners. Yes, I write on the carpeting. (This may not work for your floor. If not, skip to the next one.) Then I write numbers in the sections. Each child is responsible for cleaning his section. I often do some gerrymandering to try to make it even or to give an easier section to a younger child. We sometimes roll the dice or spin the spinner to determine the number of the section someone gets. Or I have them turn their backs, write the numbers on the section, and without them looking, have them choose a number.
+ **"Roll the Dice" or "Spin the Spinner"**: On your turn, you simply roll the dice or spin the spinner. The number that comes up is the number of objects you need to put away. Then pass the dice or spinner to someone else. Ones are a lucky spin, since you only have to put one item away.
+ **"Fill Your Bin"**: Give everyone a specific item that needs to be put away. They can either carry the bin around and put the toys in the bin or they can use a basket to gather the toys and then dump their basket into the bin. An example of this would be: "JP, you get all of the Legos. Joseph, you get the action figures. Emily, you get the kitchen toys. Jacob, you get the cars." Repeat until all the bins are full.
+ **"Get 10"**: I often hear my children using this game on their own when they've been given the job of cleaning up the room. The leader simply says, "Everyone get 10," and everyone rushes around, grabs 10 items, and puts them away. When everyone's back, the leader says again, "Everyone get 10." To mix things up a bit, the leader could change the number.
+ **"The Rake"**: (When Mom needs to help a lot.) We have a child-sized rake stored right outside our toy room. When the toys get really mixed up, I simply rake everything in the toy room into one

big pile. I sit on the floor and sort the toys into piles. Everyone puts a pile away. (This is similar to "Fill Your Bin.")

+ **"The Bribe"**: Simple and sweet. As soon as the toy room is clean, the kids can watch this TV show or play that video game until, for example, 8:00. (Putting a time limit gets kids moving more quickly, so they have more time to watch their show or play their game.)

——— A POSITIVE ATTITUDE IS CONTAGIOUS ———

When Mom and Dad have a very hopeful and happy disposition while doing the chores alongside the children, this will radically affect everyone else's attitude. Sure, we have a lot of work to do. And sure, it isn't easy. And sure, we'd all rather be doing something else. But this is our task at hand. This is what we are given to do at this moment. Reminding our children of kids in Africa who only have rocks for toys really isn't too effective. And asking them if they want some cheese to go with that whine doesn't work well, either. (Unless of course, this kind of joke lightens everyone's mood.) Smiling and joking with your kids, and just digging in to get it done, really works best. We can be demanding and strict with our children about chores without nagging and being angry ourselves. Smile and be joyful.

If you find yourself or your spouse getting frustrated or angry with the kids, or with the amount of work, call a time-out (a long bathroom break, a cup of coffee, a chore alone somewhere in the backyard, or whatever you or your spouse may need). In your time-out huddle, do what you have to do to get a paradigm shift that your family needs at this moment. For some families, Dad may need to be like a drill sergeant. Dads can usually get away with this and still seem "fun-loving." Moms, on the other hand, can come across bitchy. (Please excuse the six-letter word, but I think that word best describes it.) So beware.

One of the hardest parts of parenting is to balance the time we spend asking our kids to do something (or not to do something) with actually having conversations and fun times with them. Really, it goes back to the Mary/Martha thing again!

Look at the last eight waking hours you have had with your child. Did you spend more than half of your time saying things like, "Pick up your shoes," "Clean your room," "Don't say that," or "Put that away"? I know that our kids need to hear these things — and as parents, we need to constantly say them. But let's make sure we are balancing this practical Martha instruction with some Mary words and actions: "Did you like that book?" "How is your friend's sickness?" "What are you making?" "Can Spiderman really beat Batman?" "Let's ride bikes." And the all-time favorite: "Let's make cookies!"

If need be, the dust and fingerprints can wait until tomorrow. Trust me, they will still be there. Learning to balance the time we spend with our kids is a lifelong struggle. This is why I really like the Mary/Martha model. It serves as a constant reminder to really look at what I am doing. I constantly ask myself these simple Mary/Martha questions to help me maintain that balance:

1. *Where* is Jesus right now? Is He calling me to a quiet time of prayer? Or is He present in my child, co-worker, neighbor, or friend who is with me right now?

2. *What* does Jesus want me to do right now? Now that I have found Him, is He asking me for a quiet time of prayer? Or is He asking that I work, talk, listen, play, or (fill in the blank) *with* Him?

Asking ourselves these questions will always give us the right answer to what we should be doing and help us to live that perfectly balanced life that Mary seemed to have at that moment in the Bible.

✦ ✦ ✦

Ready for a little "home" work? Let's start with your family's cleaning plan.

Using the chart on the next page, fill in "What Needs to Be Done Daily," "What Needs to Be Done Weekly," and "What Needs to Be Done Monthly." These are the things your family needs to do in order to keep the house clean.

(Be general when you can, such as "Tidy up the family room" or "Clean the upstairs bathroom." The details of more-specific jobs will be spelled out later. If you do need specific jobs done, like "Water the plants in the sunroom," then by all means put down the specific jobs, too.)

All finished? Now that doesn't look too bad.

Your next task will be to decide who does what. If you are assigning these jobs for your kids, just put their first name initial beside their job. Put "M" for Mom on the tasks you will do ("D" for Dad). Look at them all and try to balance it out. Try it for a week or so, then set it in stone. Well, not really. But you could then put it on an official-looking chart.

What Needs to Be Done Daily	What Needs to Be Done Weekly	What Needs to Be Done Monthly

(Use chart software on your computer. Mine's on Word, and I've been using the same program for years.)

On the following page is a copy of the Kiser Family's chore chart, with room for marking our children's "shares." I just change the dates every month, print it out, and post it on our refrigerator. I know your chart will look nothing like ours — with our quirky "pay" system — but the one you make will suit your family and meet all of your cleaning needs, if you take the time to set it up and stick to it.

We have the kids write in the money they have earned on those days they do the chores. When the month is over, I total in the new amounts they have earned, and either pay them out with cash or write it on the top of the next month's chart.

✦ ✦ ✦

Sometimes you just have to dump . . .

. . . and then regroup, rebag, and reorganize!

	Seth	Michael	John Paul	Joseph	Jacob	Gabe
Daily Chores	Blue bathroom. Bedroom. Bring in dog.	Tidy up mudroom and carport. Take out trash. Bedroom. Take out dog.	Brown bathroom. Tidy up den. Bedroom. Water dog.	Downstairs bathroom. Bedroom.	Toy room. Tidy up front porch. Bedroom. Take out compost.	Clear stuff off of stairs. Bedroom. Feed cats.
Weekly Chores	Clean Glass. Clean upstairs showers. Do own laundry.	Vacuum mudroom. Tidy up yard. Do own laundry.	Vacuum stairs and hallway. Clean back patio. Put away bin of clothes.	Mop kitchen and dining room floor. Dust and vacuum den. Put away bin of clothes.	Vacuum toy room. Put away bin of clothes.	Put away bin of clothes.
	$7.00	$13.00	$7.50	$35.00	$3.00	$1.00
DATE						
Feb. 1 (Mon.)						
Feb. 4 (Thurs.)						
Feb. 6 (Sat.)						
Feb. 8 (Mon.)						
Feb. 11 (Thurs.)						
Feb. 13 (Sat.)						

Chapter 5

FROM T-BALL TO TROMBONE:

Keeping Track of Everyone's Comings and Goings

A PERFECTLY PLANNED EVENING

I arrived home with three of the older children and the baby that evening. We had spent the day two hours away in Atlanta on a homeschool field trip. I carefully planned the day so that my oldest three (all in middle school at the time) could enjoy and really benefit from our time together, away from the younger kids.

I had a friend watching the toddlers and a neighbor watching the second- and third-graders until their baseball game at 6:00 p.m. A parent of a teammate had agreed to take the second- and third-graders to the game. I also had arranged for the coach, after the game, to bring my ballplayers to the school where my husband, Keith, was still working (because of an evening program for new parents and students at the school). The kids would arrive at the

school just about when my husband's meeting was scheduled to end, and the kids knew to wait in the school's lobby. My husband was to then swing by my friend's house and gather up the toddlers there, and we would all meet at home.

When I arrived home, shortly after my husband did, I noticed something askew. It took a little while — with all the excitement of the trip, a fussy baby who had to be fed, and anxious toddlers to be settled — before realizing what was wrong. "Where are John Paul and Michael?"

My husband froze in his tracks. He just realized that they never made it to the school. But seeing how this was before we had cell phones, we quickly tried to remember what the plan had been, scrambled around for the coach's number, and gave him a call. The coach was initially speechless — and then came a million "sorrys."

My husband jumped into the car and drove to the baseball field. It was empty and dark. About five minutes after my husband left for the ball field, I got a call from the police. They had my boys. My feelings at this point were mixed — relief and joy at finding the boys, but also abject humiliation. What kind of mother was I to leave my two young boys alone in a park, at a baseball field, at night?

When my husband came home, I promptly sent him to the police station to get the boys. I couldn't show my face there. All was fine — the officers actually took the boys to get a Happy Meal at McDonald's. Needless to say, the boys thought it was great fun, police-car ride and all!

Despite the best-laid plans of mice and moms, things can go awry. Sometimes too much is too much. The one benefit of being organized on this horrific evening in the Kiser household was the speed at which I found that coach's phone number. I am hoping, though, that we can come up with some ways to help you get all those comings and goings of your family in some kind of order, and to set reasonable limitations on how many activities a family needs to have. Hopefully, you will avoid a disaster like mine, if at all possible!

KISS SOME ACTIVITIES GOOD-BYE!

Remember it is always best to KISS — Keep It Simple, Sweetie! We live in a culture that tells us to reach for more... and more... and more. When in doubt, KISS! When you feel the pressure to sign your kids up for all of those activities so that they grow up with all the advantages of the other kids, remember that there is *no substitute* for that Mary time spent between parents and kids, and between siblings.

Children who live in homes that operate as hotels and fast-food restaurants, with parents as mere chauffeurs, are not really advantaged children. They may stand a better chance at that baseball scholarship for college, but at what cost? And even that is debatable, among professionals.

Do you realize how few college athletic scholarships are actually offered? If your kid has real talent, high school (or sometimes middle school) is usually enough time to develop to the status of potential college-scholarship material in sports. I wonder why parents sacrifice so much for such meager prospects. That's not to say that kids shouldn't be in sports. I'm just saying that they don't need to be in *every* sport, nor necessarily on the traveling team.

Now, there is no way someone can tell a particular family what activities they should or should not be doing. There are far too many factors. What some consider as simple for their family, others would consider as overload. Our energy levels, our distance from events, our upbringing, our current support system (relatives, neighbors), our values or family mission, our financial situation — all of these factors determine what activities one family might choose versus another family with different circumstances. I'm going to share some general principles that may help you decide, for *your* family, which ones you need to keep or kiss good-bye:

1. **Pray.** Don't overlook this simple start to your solution. Ask God for wisdom and some clear insight. He will give it to you. Just don't be afraid to listen.

2. **Write out your schedule.** See if it is physically possible to do it. Next, judge if you can psychologically do it. Just because you can physically fit it on your calendar doesn't mean you actually have time for it. Both children and parents need downtime and completely schedule-free time.

3. **Compare your schedule to your family mission statement or your values.** "But we don't have one of these." Neither do I — nothing written down, anyway. But as a family, we have an unwritten family mission that both my husband and I have agreed upon. Writing a family mission statement is a great tool for families to do together. (Google it! There are great sites about this.) It can be the measure that you will use for all of your decisions. For us, God is the first priority. The second is one another. This already gives me some indication of what should come first. If basketball games are always on Sunday, and that is the time our family goes to church and hangs out as a family, then maybe I should look into soccer instead. If basketball is really important to us, then our family time might have to change to another day, which may mean that the ballet class has to go away. If God is first, are we involved in the parish or youth group or other activities that show this? Some other aspects of your mission statement may include service, intellect, health, the arts and music, and just plain fun. With this, you can see that school and homework take a high priority. Also, you can see how piano lessons and soccer may fit in here as well.

4. **Set a standard.** When we had all young children, we set this standard: One art (like dance, music, or drawing) and one sport per season. We have pretty much followed this as the kids have grown. And it has kept us pretty busy! Our kids have excelled in music, and we have experienced a great variety of sports. For us, to keep this standard, and to avoid not overloading our schedules, we have said no to traveling teams. We also choose not to be involved in year-round swimming, gymnastics, or a ballet company that involve a sacrifice of time and financial commitment. These work for some families, and are a great source of fun and together time, but not for us. The great variety of sports that our children have experienced — usually four different ones a year — has helped them to zone in on one or two in high school.

5. **Stick to your commitments.** I know this is difficult to do when you feel so overwhelmed and may have made a bad decision. But unless you are really desperate, try to stick it out. It teaches our children what it means to make a commitment, and what it means to be on a team. It also teaches children the virtue of fortitude. Finish those piano lessons this year (maybe you don't have to do it next year), and finish up the football season, even if you are taking a beating.

Deciding which activities to be involved in is by no means an easy process. It's a balancing act that parents have to perform. Often, both choices are right: you are okay if you do sign up for Little League, and you are okay if you don't.

Don't feel as though you are constantly on the run.

(Just a side note: By the time my third and fourth sons were ready for T-ball, I didn't sign them up. As a matter of fact, from the third son down, none of them played T-ball. It was too much for our family at the time. And generally, 5-year-olds don't really mind. They are happy just to play with Dad in the backyard. This simplified my schedule. By the time they were old enough for coach's pitch, they were still at the same playing level as the ones who had two years' "experience.")

Don't agonize too much. I think as long as you thoughtfully go through the preceding process, and keep your priorities straight, you'll usually make good decisions for your family.

SEE WHAT YOU NEED TO MANAGE

Once you have slimmed down your schedule, you'll need a system to keep track of everything that goes with these activities. And again, the simpler the system, the easier it is to use and maintain.

Before I get into some suggestions for organizing and keeping track of everyone's things, there is a simple chart I want you to fill out. By filling out this chart ahead of time, you will be able to keep your situation in mind as you read the rest of my suggestions.

Below is my chart, partially filled out. Your blank chart is at the end of this chapter, on page 136.

Activity	Who	What to Keep Track Of	How I Will Do That
Football	Michael	Practice schedule, game schedule	
Altar Serving	JP, Seth, Joseph	Schedule, list of subs	
Piano	Joseph	Practice chart, calendar, music	
Homeschool Co-op	Me	Schedule, contacts, teaching materials	
Confirmation Class	Me, JP	Workbook, teacher's book, Bible, attendance	
Youth Choir	Michael, Joseph, JP	Nothing	
Fitness Classes	Me	Schedule	
Catholic School	Seth, Michael, Joseph, JP	School calendar, handbook	
Swim Team	All	Schedules, contact lists, rules	
"Anne Frank" Play	Emily	Practice and performance schedule	
Strings Ensemble	JP, Joseph	Practice and performance schedule	

This exercise of writing down everything that you are currently "juggling" is the first step toward keeping it all organized.

EIGHT TOOLS YOU NEED TO KEEP IT TOGETHER

I am now going to go through the seven essential management tools and how you can use them to keep track of everyone's comings and goings. You already have and use many of these items. I want to challenge you to simplify the system you have so that you have better control and easier access to all of this information.

1. The Computer and/or Cell Phone With E-mail

When I started giving organizational talks 15 years ago, the computer was rarely used by the average mom for managing her home. Today, however, it is pretty hard to do this without one.

Yes, I know there are a few of you who like it the old-fashioned way. And that's fine. Many of the ways that the computer organizes things can still be done with real hard copies and real file folders. You have adapted to the computer age up to this point, so I am sure you can adapt these suggestions to your situation.

Since the computer takes up such a small space and can eliminate so much desk clutter, I highly recommend using the computer to the extent that you feel comfortable. Until pretty recently, I was recommending printing out hard copies of all the schedules and other important papers from the computer and filing them away. Anymore, however, I just suggest keeping what you need in your "Internet e-mail folders." Use these just as we used to keep file folders. Most coaches, team moms, and music teachers contact parents through the Internet.

With this in mind, create the e-mail folders you need for each activity. If you get an e-mail that you need to save (like a schedule or contact sheet), just put it in your labeled e-mail folder for that activity. My folders include: "JP's Soccer," "Seth's Soccer," "Strings Class," and "Joseph's School." Remember to clean these folders out regularly. Whenever that season or activity is through, delete — unless you think you may need that contact information for the next season. With this simple tool, you can eliminate an incredible amount of paper clutter.

If you're worried about a computer crash, remember that these aren't stored on your computer; they are stored on your e-mail servers. These usually don't crash. And in the rare case they do, you could probably find your coaches/teachers e-mails again and simply ask them to resend.

Many schedules are also kept on websites. An e-mail will probably contain such a link. Keep that e-mail with the link in the appropriate folder, or you could keep it on your "Favorite Sites."

There are many options available with computers and cell phones today. It is worth your investment in time to figure out what works best for you.

I do encourage you to take some time to keep your computer folders and e-mails streamlined. I suggest that you keep only as many e-mails as will fill one page. When you have to go to page 2, you have too many. Delete, delete, delete . . . and on occasion, put it in an e-mail folder.

2. Calendar

Another way the computer can help you organize is the calendar. The first things we want on our calendars are the dates and times of all our activities. Using a computer is easiest for this. If you have Boy Scouts every Wednesday night at 6:00, you only have to type it once and it will appear for every Wednesday. If you have Music Club the first Tuesday of every month, you only need to type it once and it appears for you each month. We can easily see if we have any conflicts in our schedules.

The biggest complaint I hear from mothers about keeping calendars is the problem of copying the events from one calendar to the next. Some moms like to have a calendar on their computer, a calendar in the kitchen for everyone to see, and a calendar to carry with them in their purse. To solve this problem, I primarily use my computer calendar. When I need additional copies for my planner or the bulletin board, I simply print copies.

I have used Outlook, Google, Yahoo, and Cozi calendars. I have liked them all, but I am currently using Cozi.com because it syncs (synchronizes) other calendars onto it easily; for instance, if someone uses a particular computer calendar for the sports schedule, I can add it to my Cozi calendar without having to copy all of the dates. I also like the Cozi calendar because it has a section for all my "To Do" lists; for example, I have a BOC (Big and Occasional Chores) list, a "Honey Do" list, and a "To Do Today" list). Cozi also color-codes the events by person. Many online calendars do these same things. And most are free! (In the unlikely event any of these calendar providers go out of business or begin to charge a fee, I just hope the provider gives me some kind of warning so that I can make a hard copy of the year or transfer everything to another one.)

Cell phones are also a great place for your calendar. Many women use their phones in the same way that I use my Cozi calendar. It works the same way.

As I mentioned earlier, another benefit of using a computer is the ability to make copies. I make monthly copies to go into my planner and on our bulletin board. This copy on the bulletin board is for the entire family to see. It tells us who the altar server will be this weekend, who has a game tonight, when we are going camping, and when the school play is. If I have to add something new to this current month, I first add it to the computer calendar. Often this is done from an e-mail. When I read my e-mail, I have my calendar open on another tab, ready to add to it. A benefit of having your e-mail the same as your calendar (such as a Yahoo calendar) is that it adds these dates at a single click. If it's only a change for this current month's calendar posted on my bulletin board, I will simply pencil it in. If I have a lot of these add-ons, I will print out a new calendar for the month and for my planner. By the way, some of these web-based calendars also sync to your phone, whether it has Internet capabilities or not.

The key is to keep your calendar (in whatever form) accurate and up-to-date. If you are using both the phone and your computer, make sure they automatically sync or that you regularly sync them. I always check my computer calendar first thing in the morning. I look at my "To Do Today" list and see what I need to do for the day. I also look ahead for the week so that I know what's coming.

3. Bulletin Board

One of those computer-generated calendars is posted to an area designated for our bulletin board. It doesn't necessarily have to be a bulletin board, but for ease of adding and removing, a cork bulletin board is recommended.

I have the calendar in the lower center. Above the calendar, I have two "chore" charts. The top circular chart is the one that rotates for the dinner chores. (In the previous chapter, we talked about the kids' chores.) In the top-right corner, I have a list of family prayer concerns that we try to remember when we pray.

Between the dinner-chore wheel and the prayer concerns, we have a very specific spot for invitations. Invitations are placed here after they

My bulletin board.

are recorded on the calendar and a note has been made to purchase a gift or RSVP if needed. I like to keep them so that I can easily double-check the date and time, directions, dress code, etc.

Under the prayer concerns, I have a folder for restaurant coupons so that when we order out, I've got the most recent ones. (I keep grocery store coupons in my purse.)

In the top left, I keep the most recent church bulletin. When I come home from church each Sunday, I toss out the old bulletin and put up the new.

Under the church bulletin, I keep a stack of schedules/calendars. These are mostly calendars that have too many dates to record onto my computer calendar. A good example of a calendar I keep here is the workout calendar from the gym. I don't want to keep track of every class they offer, but I need to check this when I am looking for a class I want to attend. I also keep complicated schedules, such as my daughter's play-practice schedule, in this "stack." I don't write these practices on my calendar — she can keep track of them — but I have a copy if I want to check when they are. Mind you, all of these can be found electronically, but it is convenient for me to have them at my fingertips in the kitchen. It's on a side wall going into my food pantry, easily available but not in clear view to clutter up my kitchen.

4. Your Planner

Your planner choice is really dependent on your style and personality. With the amount of organizing and storing our computers and phones can do for us, we now have less and less reliance on a traditional planner. For me, my planner serves as a "go-between" and a "hold me over" until I get back to my computer at my desk. For this reason, I have chosen a smaller planner that can easily be carried around.

I keep the lists in it that I might need to use when I am mobile. Some of these are: movies I want to rent, prayer concerns (so that if someone asks me to pray for someone, I can pull out my planner and write it down), goals, and things I want to purchase on sale (if, for example, I see an end table at a yard sale). I have a current calendar folded in here as well.

Today, many cell phones offer the same services as a full-scale traditional planner. If you have one with these capabilities, it could be a saw-sharpening experience to figure out how to use all that it has to offer.

5. Purse

My purse is the next topic because the planner is stored inside here. I consider my purse to be my briefcase. It carries my planner, cell phone (when I don't have pockets), coupons, wallet, mini-photo album, and zipper pouches. When I had an infant in tow, I used a diaper bag for this or a purse that was large enough to carry a couple of diapers and travel-sized wipes. (Why is it that the more children you have, the smaller your diaper bag becomes?)

One of my best ideas for my purse has been to carry a mini-photo album — not for photos, but to organize some of the bulky stuff that I had been trying to stuff into my wallet. Each photo sleeve has a different category. One category is credit cards. In here, I keep my extra credit cards, such as my store credit cards. I do try not to have too many of these cards; but the few I have are kept in this photo pocket.

In another photo pocket, I keep my gift cards and tickets. This one has a few restaurant gift cards, tickets to an upcoming symphony, and leftover store gift cards from Christmas. I never have to say, "Darn, here I am at this store, but the gift card is at home in a drawer" or "Did you bring the tickets, honey?"

Another pocket is for library cards. Another contains our health insurance card. Still another is for membership cards to the zoo, the motor club, the science center, and so forth.

The one category of cards that is the most annoying to try to keep in a small wallet is the store discount card. These are the cards the store cashier scans in order for you to get certain discounts or keep track of bonus points. As you know, most grocery stores and some retail stores use these cards. I keep the one I use most on my key chain. The rest go in the photo album pocket. I use another photo pocket for punch cards.

I use yet another pocket for prescriptions and doctor-appointment cards, after I have put the appointment on my calendar; it's nice to keep these cards in case I need to contact a doctor. The phone number and address are usually on these business-like cards.

What is really convenient about the mini-photo album is that you can customize it any way that suits you. My actual wallet is very small and just has my license, bank card, and one credit card. You can see how easy it is for me to use this system when I go to the store. I don't have to shuffle through a big wallet, looking for what I need. I mostly just use this small wallet. And if I do happen to need something in my photo/"card" organizer, I simply pull it out and flip to the right page and pull out what I need. Many of my seminar participants have tried this idea and like it very much.

Here is another great organization idea for your purse: zipper pencil pouches. These come in a variety of styles and usually are on sale at back-to-school time. These usually have a clear side and have grommets that make them attachable in a binder. I have fashionable all-fabric ones with zippers, which I use to organize the miscellaneous odds and ends that I like to carry around in my purse.

If you have seen those "organized" purses, with a million pockets, that sling over the shoulder, this zipper-pouch idea is similar to using one of those. The difference is that you can customize your purse to whatever pockets and sections you need. And you can use these in whatever style of purse you want. Using zipper pouches also makes it very easy for when you want to switch purses. All you have to do is grab your zipper pouches, your planner, your wallet, coupon holder, and your mini-photo/"card" album and put them into your other purse.

I try to have nothing "floating loose" in my purse. I use the pockets on the sides to hold just a small wallet, cell phone, and checkbook. The rest of my stuff is categorized and stored in one of these zipper pouches. I only have three that I use. You may want more or less.

One is for receipts; I found it easy just to pop all my receipts into one of these. Another one is for "health and beauty"; this pouch has lip balm, a compact, adhesive bandages, Ibuprofin, a maxi pad, safety pins, etc. In my last pouch I have: a couple of photographs, a watch that needs a new battery, and a check. Can you guess what category this is? This is my "To Do" pouch. When I need to return something to someone or get something fixed, I put it in here. I was tired of finding things on the bottom of my purse that I was supposed to have given to somebody. Now I know I just need to look at this pocket to see what needs to be done when I go out.

A purse like this is great when you go to a store for a small, simple purchase: you simply pull out the small wallet that has one debit card and a license in it. No more digging through your whole purse. Or how about having to find that rare store credit card that you use three times a year, but if you use it today you get an extra 20 percent off? It's in the mini-photo/"card" album, in its appropriate sleeve. And finally, you notice that somebody needs to trim his nails when you are on your way to church. That's easy. The nail clippers are in the zipper pouch for "health and beauty."

I like to encourage women not to worry if their purse seems disarrayed. If you don't have time to put something into the zipper pouch, just

throw it into the purse. If you are like most women, you'll have time to sort through your purse while waiting at the dentist or in the carpool line or during a slow inning of a baseball game.

Use these times to reorganize and clean out your purse and zipper pouches. Or look through your planner. Or clean out your car. Or throw out expired coupons. Smart Marthas try to use this kind of time wisely.

Here is my purse with my card organizer and a zipper pouch.

6. Desk With Bins and Files

I am blessed to have a large desk with a file cabinet near it. I think all women need some kind of space like this to keep papers and files in order. Many women today have nice desks with computers right in their kitchen. If you don't mind a little activity while you are working, and since most kitchens are the activity center of the house, a desk and computer work great here.

You need three bins or collection spots at your desk. These could be baskets, drawers, or a combination of whatever:

✦ **"Action Bin"**: This first bin collects papers that I need to act upon. I like to use a clear, upright, magazine holder for this stuff. (I found that when I put these papers into a drawer, I tended to let it build up.) I also keep this right on my desk so that I am always looking at it.

✦ **"Children's Memento Bin"**: In my case, I actually use a dish basin, which I keep at the back of a drawer in my desk. In here, I collect all my children's precious mementos. These are papers, newspaper clippings, photos, really good artwork, certificates, and anything else that I want to keep for my children. Remember to be discerning about what you want to save when you collect it. I will tell you in the next chapter how I deal with this memorabilia. I empty this bin about once a year.

✦ **"Bill Bin"**: Here I simply collect the bills that have to be paid. (Yes, we are doing most of this online now. I think we will be paying all of them electronically soon.) The other thing that this bin collects is our charity donations. We keep our church envelopes in here, as well as other requests for charitable donations. At the end of each month, we take the money we had designated for charitable giving and divvy it up between these requests. (Let me make a simple plea with you right now to have some kind of budget system in place. This is an important part of being responsible with the money God has given you. If you need to work on this, put it at the top of your BOC list. We like both Phil Lenahan and his Veritas Financial Ministries [*www.VeritasFinancialMinistries.com*] and Dave Ramsey [*www.DaveRamsey.com*].)

The reason I designate these bins and places for these papers is because it is very important to NEVER LET THINGS PILE UP. If you have places for everything, this is less likely to happen. Of course, these bins and baskets can also pile up, so it is important to keep after these piles — constantly! There is no way around it.

My clear "action" bin.

Just because you have stuff in a bin, doesn't mean it is "organized." Only use bins or baskets for the things you need. For example, don't have a bin of used magazines — unless it is in your craft stuff for your children to cut up. Remember, if you can't read the magazine in one month's time, then maybe you should lighten your subscriptions. We toss (recycle) those magazines and newspapers once the next issue comes. If there is something in the old magazine you want to keep, tear it out and file it — but only if you are really going to use it again. The only things I will file from magazines are recipes — and I put these into a recipe binder. Most magazines are now online. You have access to all of their archives, so don't save the hard copies.

Files

Since I am not filing magazine articles, what kinds of files do I have? I have two kinds of files. The first kind is what I call the *important files*. These are files for papers you need to keep and access occasionally. Some examples are: insurance papers, copies of deeds and birth certificates, health records, tax documents, warranties, and copies of service and maintenance work.

I don't think any elaborate system is needed here. I use basic labeled manila folders. Keep them cleaned out when things go out of date.

I have received the suggestion many times from the women at my seminars that some of these files need an emergency backup. I recently copied some important documents and a few credit cards to keep in my small fireproof safe, with some of those other important documents, like deeds, birth certificates, titles, will, and recent passports. One woman at a recent seminar said that she put this copied information in a sealed brown envelope for safekeeping at her best friend's house. What we are safeguarding here are documents that might be destroyed in the unlikely event of a fire or flood. Do you know all your insurance companies? Where are your savings? Just think for a minute of all the information you'd have to find elsewhere if your important files were destroyed, and that will give you some idea of what you want in the fireproof safe.

The reason for copying the credit cards is in case you lose your purse, as happened to a good friend of mine recently. She showed up at my house in tears because someone had stolen her purse. We had to think of all the credit cards she had and look up all the numbers online. It didn't take as long as I thought it would, but how much easier this would have been if she had kept actual copies of all the credit cards and bank cards. If you have a copy machine at home, just take a moment to pull all of these out of your purse and copy them. Keep one copy in your important files and the other copy in your safe. Now, don't you feel more protected already?

The other category of files that I have at my desk I call *activity files*. Not to be confused with the "action bin," these files are where I am putting the information I want to have hard copies of. Some of these files I can probably eliminate simply by using our computer folders. But for some activities, I may need more than just a schedule to keep. Those activities get a folder in the activity files.

For example, our son is in football. We were given some papers about team guidelines, schedules, directions to the games, and a roster. These go into a folder labeled "Football." I have a school folder, which contains the St. Joseph's School handbook and calendar. I have a child with asthma. He gets a folder here to keep track of his many prescriptions.

You may need many of these — or like me, very few. Many moms have used three-ring binders for files and papers like these. This is the same idea, but just stored in a binder instead. They often keep this binder in the kitchen by their phone. Another mom I met recently uses an accordion file for these same types of files. She keeps it in her kitchen and pulls it out when needed.

When younger-aged children attend school, we have to deal with all of their papers from school. Many teachers provide a folder for their students. When I had younger children in school, I just kept their folder and papers in the backpack. I kept the papers that I would need to refer to in the future in the activity file at my desk, labeled with the name of their school. Most of the papers were either immediately signed and put back in the folder in the backpack, to be returned to school, or were secretly pitched.

There are many things that you probably shouldn't file. In the past, I used to file many magazine articles, catalogs, and travel brochures. Today, most magazine articles, as I said already, can be found online when you need them. Catalogs are also online.

You can save yourself so much clutter and piles by eliminating much of the stuff we used to save. I do still save some travel brochures, if I know I will use them again. As you can see, this is a matter of preference. I just encourage you to KISS with your files.

7. Bags

There is one other organizational tool that some of you might find useful. Bags? Yes, simple canvas bags. Often you can get these for free at conferences. Or you can buy them for a song at craft stores. I have found many great uses for these inexpensive bags.

One I use as a "Meeting in a Bag." I found that, for some activities I was involved in, I had not only papers to keep track of, but also some other materials, such as books. So I decided to keep the papers in a file or binder and keep them in the bag along with the books. I no longer needed anything in a file at my desk.

This was great for when I taught a confirmation class at my church. I had teacher's books, a Bible, attendance sheets, forms, schedules, etc. I just put all of this stuff in a bag. I called it my "Confirmation bag." Whenever I had to plan the class, I just grabbed my bag, went to a quiet spot, and had all my stuff right there. Whenever it was time to go to the class, I just grabbed my bag and went. No need to scramble around making sure I had everything.

I also have a "Co-op bag." This is for our homeschool co-op. I teach one of the classes and keep everything in this bag. If I have to remember to take something to the co-op, I just put it in the bag, and it gets there!

I keep my "bags" in my hall closet.

I also have a "Dance bag." This is for the dance classes that I teach. It not only has rosters, dance notes, and an iPod, but it also has tap and ballet shoes.

The final bag I use is not a cheap canvas bag, but one of those smaller luggage bags with wheels. Every couple of months I am called to teach an NFP (natural family planning) class at my church. Many papers, files, and materials are needed for that, including a projector. I don't really need much preparation for the class because I've been teaching it for years. So when it's time to teach, I just pull the handle and wheel it to the car.

Okay. Now the secret is out as to how I can do many activities like these and always have what I need.

8. Other Lists and Memo Boards

I highly suggest that every family put a "Things to Buy" list at a very convenient place in their home. Ours is on the side of our refrigerator.

Not only do I use this when we run out of baking powder, but my older children also use this list to write down personal items like deodorant or shaving cream, when they run out. My husband uses it, too. If the kids need something for school, like a science board, they are responsible for getting it on the list. I even take special requests on this list: everything from Ho Hos to a particular brand of shampoo. I'm not obliged to purchase their requests, but it's nice to know what they like. "Who knows," I say, "it may be on sale."

Being disciplined about using this simple list will save many extra shopping trips. When it's time for me to go to the store, I grab the list off the refrigerator and tuck it into my planner.

As far as lists and mail that belong to the kids, I always thought that those cubbyholes, like those in offices and schools, would be neat to have in my kitchen. I didn't have the space to spare for something like this, and I wasn't sure how much I would use it. So when I saw memo/dry-erase boards on sale at a price too good to pass up, I bought eight of these for my family. I decided that I would use these as each child's message center. I store them all on the side of my refrigerator. When I need to leave a message for one of my children, I simply put the message on their board and place it on the front of the refrigerator. These kinds of boards work very well for me because they also can hold envelopes and other pieces of mail. So essentially, they are like those cubbyholes that hold mail, but with the bonus of being message boards as well. After a child receives his mail or a message, he then places his memo board back on the side.

What I especially like about this system is that it serves as a reminder for me to deliver the message. I see it on the front of the refrigerator, and I remind that child to take a look. It also works great for those busy teens who are always on the go. I don't want to bark reminders at my teen when I get to see him for only five minutes that day. Instead, I can say things like, "How was that geometry test?" or "Does your ankle still hurt at practice?" — and "Did you check your memo board?" Meanwhile, his memo board has a reminder for him to get his clothes out of the dryer, to put his shoes away, to turn in the permission form for the youth-group bowling night that is attached to the memo board, and another letter from a prospective college.

Instead of memo boards on the refrigerator, you could use personalized magnets or magnetic clips. By "personalized," I mean name or initials written with a Sharpie marker. (We have a lot of personalized items in our home labeled this way.) These could hold mail, messages on sticky notes, and so on. Or there's the more traditional way of using one memo board and addressing it with the name of whoever is receiving the message. Less space and money are invested, but it's the same idea.

If I have things that are too big to go on the memo board, I will either use my children's stair or laundry bin, as I mentioned earlier.

BACK TO OUR CHARTS

Here is my completed chart, showing how I've stored and organized some of our family's activities:

Activity	Who	What to keep track of	How I will do that
Football	Michael	Practice schedule, game schedule	Activity file, computer e-mail file
Altar Servers	JP, Seth, Joseph	Schedule, list of subs	Computer e-mail file
Piano	Joseph	Practice chart, calendar, music	Bag for Joseph, calendar on bulletin board
Homeschool Co-op	Me	Schedule, contacts, teaching materials	Bag
Confirmation Class	Me, JP	Workbook, teacher's book, Bible, attendance	Bag
Youth Choir	Michael, Joseph, JP	Nothing	Nothing
Fitness Classes	Me	Schedule	Bulletin board
Catholic School	Seth, Michael, Joseph, JP	School calendar, handbook	Activity file
Swim Team	All	Schedules, contact lists, rules	Computer e-mail file
"Anne Frank" Play	Emily	Practice and performance schedule	Bulletin board
Strings Ensemble	JP, Joseph	Practice and performance schedule	Computer e-mail file

Now is the time to look over your chart. If you are using some methods that work for you, then great! Tweak them and continue to use them. Maybe you can combine some of your ideas with mine, or even come up with new ones. If you want a complete overhaul, then go for it! Start with your chart, a good calendar, and a planner.

CONCLUSION: MAKING A HOUSE A HOME, NOT A HOTEL AND RESTAURANT

My experience with most hotels and restaurants is that they are very efficient organizations. I don't see piles of messy papers stacked up, and I don't see attendants scurrying about looking for misplaced bills. If they weren't efficient and orderly, they wouldn't stay in business.

However, our homes are not hotels and restaurants. Being able to handle a very full schedule of carpooling children to and fro, seven days a week, even though it can be "managed," may mean our home is sometimes like a hotel. But just because we are able to do something, may not mean that we should. It may be too much. Here are some warnings for those of us who tend to be like Martha and run a tight ship.

No one really likes staying in a hotel for too long. Oh sure, it's nice for the first few days. But there is something about a home that we long to go to. To be neat and orderly is nice — and all this helps to make our house livable — but it only goes so far toward making our house a home. Having things structured and in order is just a tool that makes it easier for us to be the parents we want to be, and to have that nurturing home. Let's remember that structure and order are not our ends.

Martha could run a hotel or restaurant. Mary could run a home. Even if you can manage to "make it work," is it really *all* that you want?

✦ ✦ ✦

Now it's your turn to organize your family's activities, using the chart on the next page.

Activity	Who	What to Keep Track Of	How I Will Do That

MEMORIES... IN THE CORNER OF OUR CLOSET:

Collecting and Storing Memorabilia

Dummm, dee, da–dum, daaa, daaa. Dah, dee, da-dum, dah. I'm "singing" *Pomp and Circumstance*, the graduation song, in case you didn't follow my intonations. I've seen three of my children march down the aisle in their cap and gown to this tune. Before you know it, if you haven't experienced this yet, you will. And I'm sure you've been told this so many times before: how quickly time passes, and how you need to treasure these moments, blah, blah, blah. And yet, many of us still spend our time looking ahead to better days and greener pastures.

Our third graduation.

THE MAGIC STRING

This reminds me of a story I usually tell at my seminars. It's an old story about a boy who finds a "magic string." He realizes that it's magic one day when he finds himself being chased by a group of older boys who want to beat him up. He pulls a little on the string — and swish! — he is magically transported to his home that evening, sitting down to dinner with his family. He pulls the string on many other occasions and realizes that when he does, he is immediately transported to a future time. He then tucks the string away, only to be used for emergency situations, lest the magic wears out.

The boy becomes a young man and gets a young wife. The first years of marriage are a little rocky, with some fighting and stress over finances.

He gets the string out, pulls it — and swish! — he is several months ahead, at a peaceful time with his wife. When they have their first baby, the child is sick and colicky. He grows tired of hearing the cries; he is just plain tired. So he gets his string out — and swish! — it is months later, and all is better.

As additional children come along — and with illnesses, job stresses, and the ordinary stresses of life weighing in — he finds himself turning to the string more and more. Finally, he pulls the string one more time — and he finds himself to be an old man, lying on his deathbed.

He had always envisioned that, at this moment, he would pass the string along to his children so that they, too, could have an easy life. But instead, he asks his son to take the old piece of string from his hands and throw it into the fire. For you see, he now realizes that he didn't really live life.

Don't "Pull Your String"

In all your drama, stress, tiredness, and inconveniences, I just want to encourage all mothers of infants, toddlers, tweens, and teens to stop "pulling your string."

I can remember so many times in my life when I longed for the days when I could "sleep through the night," because I had infants who thought it was normal to eat in the middle of the night. Or I'd long for the time when I would be "out of diapers." I have dreamed of times when I could travel without a diaper bag and stroller, and when I could eat at a restaurant, at a leisurely pace, enjoying real conversation. Or maybe I'm dreading time in carpool lines. Or, as a mom with tweens, perhaps I'm wanting to have a quiet Friday night at home, without having to worry and check on what movie they're watching or what activity they're doing at someone's house. How about with teens? (If you think that will be easy for you... well, if it turns out that way, you'll be one of the lucky few!) Have you stayed up half the night because someone has broken curfew, thinking: "Will I ever get a good night's sleep again?"

At most stages of life, there are times when we'd all love to "pull the string" — looking forward to "better days," instead of living and embracing what we have in front of us. When we long and dream for what is to come, we run the risk of missing all that life has to offer us now. It's just like "pulling the string."

With the passing of time, our memories accumulate and so does the memorabilia that call to mind the important moments and accomplishments of our children's lives. These mementos, which we are going to talk about next, are a wonderful way to reminisce about our children growing up, but they are in no way a substitute for enjoying those children now. I'd even say that if collecting and storing mementos in any way takes away from enjoying your children in the present moment, please enjoy what is going on now and don't worry about trying to capture the memory with some memento.

MEMORABILIA SHOULD NOT BE STRESSFUL

Now that we have established that real life is better than a record of it, we can start to look at what kind of record we should keep.

Of course, less is more. Having fewer items that are meaningful and easy to access and view is, in my view, more fulfilling than having a humongous collection, in the long run. If you've ever had the experience of looking through boxes of your parents' photos, trying to guess who is who, and then trying to decide what to do with these, you know how overwhelming this can be.

I've also experienced going through boxes of my parents' slides and old movies. Although it was a lot of fun to see movies of myself when I was 3, it was also time-consuming, and a little stressful, trying to figure out what to do with it all. And yes, my father is now in the process of transferring them to DVD. I guess this is something to do when you're retired. I'd like to save my dependents (and myself) from that hassle, and at the same time be able to enjoy some of those videos with my children before they reach 40. (Even now, my teens love to see videos of themselves when they were 3. It is a good reminder for them to see how 3-year-olds act, so they won't get so frustrated with their younger siblings.)

The system I use for storing memorabilia is simple, yet it seems thorough enough to be more than sufficient. There are basically three ways that I store our precious memories: photos, videos, and individual memorabilia boxes.

1. PHOTOS: A PICTURE'S WORTH A THOUSAND WORDS

Since this is the case, you really don't need too many. Luckily, with digital photos, we can store so many in such a small space.

When we first started our family, we didn't have digital photos. I found myself making doubles at every developing. I'd keep a set of the good ones, and then I would divide that second set among the children. Mine went into the family photo albums. Theirs went chronologically into a small file box that they kept in their individual memorabilia boxes.

As you can imagine, I treasure these photos. In case of a house fire, it's women and children (and husband, of course), photo albums, and then pets — in that order. I mention this because I know that some of you may still have boxes of photos that need to be sorted. You will treasure these, but only if you take the time to label and put them into albums. Be selective here as well. Save no extras of the same picture or bad shots. Sort the extras for your kids' collections in their memento boxes. To get this done, put this on your BOC (Big and Occasional Chores) list. Make this your movie-viewing activity. Or your Sunday afternoon activity. It won't take you as long as you think.

In our family, all of our photos are now taken digitally. I don't handle nearly as many hard copies (photographs) as in the past. I still have an updated family photo album, but it has very selected shots — and I don't even bother printing any photos for the kids' memento boxes anymore. I use an online photo service (such as Snapfish, Shutterfly, or Walmart — there are many others to choose from) for backup, storage, and printing selected photos. These services, as well as many others, let you share photos very easily by e-mail to friends, family, and even to Facebook. If you have ever tried to attach a large number of photos to an e-mail, you know that this is time-consuming for both the sender and the receiver. This is why I recommend sharing photos with an online service. And yes, most are free.

Since my photos are saved on my computer by date, I categorize my pictures for easy reference by month and year. Once a month, I download all of my pictures to Snapfish and save them by that month's name — such as "January 2010" — onto a Snapfish album. That now makes three stored copies of these pictures: the first is on my personal computer, the second is on the Internet site, and the third is on the SD card in my camera. And because I back up my hard drive, I have a reliable fourth copy as well. This seems pretty safe to me.

But I also go ahead and order hard copies of my favorite pictures. These favorites, as I said, go into the family album. If I don't have enough to print from one month, sometimes I'll wait until I have more to order, or usually I wait for a sale. Now I have a fifth copy of some of my pictures.

In addition to this, I download these pictures onto CDs once a year. Why bother with this step? Did I mention that I made nine of these CDs?

Yes, there is one for each child, to be stored in his memorabilia box. They each have a small CD album stored in their memorabilia box, which will hold thousands of pictures stored on CDs. This method is relatively simple for me to do — and then each of my children has a copy of all the photos from his or her childhood. Simple-and-consistent keeps me up-to-date with all of my photos. My children (and their children) will thank me someday.

2. LIGHTS, CAMERA, ACTION — VIDEO!

I haven't quite figured out when to shoot videos, or when to take photos, or when I should do both. Usually, I grab my camera. But if it is something that involves motion or music, or funny antics, I'll go for the video.

Capturing those first baby steps on video is priceless. One of our favorite videos we ever made as a family shows us catching a copperhead snake, *Crocodile Hunter*-style, in our garage and releasing it in a faraway field. Because video is a little more tedious to sort through (and sometimes boring, except to moms), and since it's time-consuming to edit, let me encourage you to be selective when filming. With photos, you can shoot lots and easily dump them; for most of us, this is not the case with videos.

That said, we still have our share of home videos, and there is really nothing quite like a moving picture with sound to help reminisce about another time. Since they take up so much memory on the computer, *for now* I store my videos on DVDs. And just like the photos, I make each family member a copy of all the family videos. I have a DVD burner to do this. Many computers have this capability. These family DVDs are also stored in each child's CD album, in his memorabilia box. The system is simple: When the mini-tape gets full on my video camera, I immediately transfer the videos onto ten DVDs (nine for each child and one for me.)

Sure, I realize that media storage is going to change. I had to transfer all of my old VCR tapes onto DVDs. And those DVDs will all have to be transferred someday to another kind of storage device. But just as there was technology available to transfer all of those VCR tapes to DVDs, I know that technology will also be available for my kids to use in a future transfer.

Sharing and Storing Pictures Elsewhere

I love to see a "growing family portrait gallery" when I visit elderly couples' homes. What I mean by this is the progressive display of family portraits that starts with the wedding picture. Then we see the young

141

couple and their first baby. Next we see a baby and toddler with Mom and Dad. The following picture chronicles Mom and Dad and more children. Finally, after many additions, we see that picture of Grandma and Grandpa, their grown children with their spouses, and all of the grandchildren. What started as a single couple has developed into a tribe. I love it!

To create your own "growing family portrait gallery," you wouldn't necessarily need to have a picture of every year, but maybe a total of six or seven. This is something you can think about as you are planning to decorate your walls. And I never get rid of past family portraits. I simply store mine behind current pictures I have on display. I switch them around from time to time, when I get the chance.

I haven't started my "growing family portrait gallery" yet, but simply have some random family portraits around. I will work on this. What I have currently on display are eight-by-tens of each of my children's most recent pictures, arranged neatly on a wall. Yes, it is very hard to keep all of these current. I usually use the occasion of birthdays to get their pictures taken. If they attend school, I just use their school picture. All of their previous portraits are stored behind the current one. This wall attracts visitors that come into our home, as we introduce our children. This is to the relief of our children, since it beats blowing the whistle and lining them up to say their names, Von Trapp style.

I also have ten-by-thirteens of all our children when they were 3 months old. These line the wall going up the stairs, in birth order, in case anyone needs to figure out who is who. We call it "The Baby Hallway of Fame."

A final idea for pictures is to display them in photo collages. This is a fun and inexpensive way to decorate a wall. Our children's friends really enjoy seeing the Kisers in younger days, and in unusual places, such as pumpkin farms and bathtubs. I also like collages that run on a theme. We are trying to start one with homes of famous people. So far we have several, including pictures of us at the homes of Samuel Clemens (Mark Twain) and Thomas Edison.

Other ideas for a family photo collage collection would be of distant relatives that aren't seen very often, waterfalls of South Carolina (or lighthouses, bridges, battlefields, etc.), or even those roller coaster pictures that are taken at amusement parks. The photo collage that you compile, even if it is just "Famous Graves of Our State," will be the envy of the neighborhood.

3. THOSE MEMORABILIA BOXES

Let me take you on a journey through one of our children's "memorabilia boxes." I've heard some moms call something like this a "treasure box." Well, in addition to this memorabilia box, our kids also have a treasure box. Their treasure box is different because they control what is saved in it. This is the box of those "special" toys that I allow them to store in their rooms. It also contains "valuables," like kid's meal toys, rocks, and bird feathers. Their memorabilia box contains treasures of another kind — but unlike their treasure box, they aren't allowed to play with it when they are young.

First of all, I will describe our memorabilia boxes. They are simply Rubbermaid bins. Some kids have the under-the-bed size. Others have a little larger version. The goal is to only save enough memorabilia that can be easily stored in this bin.

In case you are wondering how I am storing and organizing all of this stuff before it goes into the bins, remember what I said about the bin in my desk drawer. I collect all of the children's memorabilia in that bin under my desk for about a year. After a year, I sort the bin's contents into nine separate piles. I simply deliver these piles to all the bins and put the items in their respective places in the bin. And yes, this is a pain to do, but I figure that it's worth the hassle to ensure that my children have a nice collection of childhood mementos stored. Here is what is inside my oldest son's bin:

1. **CD/DVD album:** I already mentioned this.
2. **File box with photos:** Just my older five have this.
3. **Baby book/baby calendar.**
4. **Document-sized (or larger) pocket file folder:** This is the kind that has an elastic string that loops around the outside to keep it closed. Any kind of multiple file folder would work. Mine has five large pockets inside. I've labeled these: "Newspaper Clippings," "Artwork," "Certificates and Programs," "Special Papers/ Letters," and "Other." It's like a mini-file for these papers, only mine is slightly larger than a regular file folder. If you can't find one that's big enough, use the regular-sized pocket folder for everything except the artwork, and use an artist portfolio for the artwork. The idea is to try to keep a little order to these kinds of papers and pictures. This material, along with photos, would ideally go into a scrapbook.

5. **Scrapbook.** I had started a scrapbook once. It's kept in here. It's nothing like the elaborate scrapbooks that people make today. I am not a scrapbooker, but I do really love them. If we ever had the opportunity to have a nicer scrapbook made for him, we would have all of the material organized and ready in the pocket folder.

6. **Our Christmas newsletters:** I store these in a red pocket folder with fasteners. We started doing a family Christmas newsletter when he was 3. We are up to 17 newsletters in this folder, and they read like a family history. Every Christmas, I just make sure that I have nine extra copies ready for everyone's memento box. I three-hole-punch them and keep them in the memento bin, in my desk drawer, until I'm ready to move them into the children's memento bin.

7. **School memories book:** Perhaps you had one of these when you were in school. I don't see them around too much anymore. It's a book of pocket pages that you fill out, tape your school picture onto, and put your report card in the pocket. I found these at a grocery store one year and bought five of them. Since my younger children do not have these books, I just put their report cards and other test results into the "other" pocket in the pocket

Each child has a pocket folder for every year's Christmas newsletter.

folder. If I have leftover school pictures, they are stored with the other portraits.

8. **Portraits:** I keep one folder/envelope with leftover portraits. I will mostly never use all of these, but I don't have the heart to throw them out. If you ever purchased that 52-piece portrait special at Walmart or Sears, then you know what I'm talking about!

9. **Extra stuff:** I have some extra items in my son's bin that I simply store in Ziploc bags. One bag has a couple of G.I. Joes, which he loved to play with. One has a favorite Beanie Baby. One has a postcard collection. And yet another has some ribbons and medals. In his brother's memento bin, I have extras like a baby outfit in a food-storage bag, an orthodontic mouth plaster caste, X rays, a coin collection, and a special baseball. A certain number of objects like this can make the bin very special, but don't get carried away. If you had a very, very important trophy, it could also be included. Note that I am not a big fan of trophies, unless they are given out for truly significant events.

Our oldest son's memorabilia box.

10. **High-school diploma:** Drumroll, please!

This may look slightly messy, but it does the job. The lid gets put on it, and it is stored on a shelf in the closet. It's easy to get to when needed. And when he is settled in his future home with his future wife and family, the bin will be moved there.

OTHER MEMORABILIA STORAGE IDEAS

Storing Electronically

I met one woman who took pictures of all her children's memorabilia and then simply stored the photos on her computer. She took pictures of their artwork, certificates (with the children holding them), trophies (again with the kids holding them), and so on. This is a great idea for limiting the amount of stuff you have to store. It completely cuts the clutter. What would be "worth more" in the future: a picture of your child in uniform holding his Little League trophy or a dusty plastic trophy? Even large pieces of artwork that would later turn brown and fray on the edges could be easily captured by a photo.

I haven't gone completely this way, because there is something I like about holding and seeing the "real" thing. But I am certainly using this option more and more. You could even print out these pictures for a photo album/scrapbook that would be stored in your child's memorabilia box.

A Rotating Gallery

I personally don't like a lot of clutter on my refrigerator. I usually post a picture for a day or two, then get rid of it. If your refrigerator has a lot of photos, magnets, and pictures on it, try this test: put all of this in a file folder and store it with your other files temporarily. Now, doesn't your kitchen seem a lot cleaner? Maybe yours doesn't, but mine always does. Does that slight sense of feeling cleaner outweigh the feeling you get looking at your photos and children's artwork? If so, then find a place for all of the pictures you took off. If not, then put them back on the refrigerator. For me, I have found that I really like that clutter-free look in my kitchen, so I try to keep my refrigerator clear (except for an occasional memo board that I mentioned in the previous chapter).

So as to not scandalize my children by disregarding their artwork, I found another way to display it. I call it my "rotating gallery." I have simply found a wall where I can tape and retape their artwork. I've been in homes where the moms have actually had some of their children's artwork framed. I love this.

Along these same lines, I met one mom who had random frames on the wall in which she could easily change the artwork. This is a fancier variation of my rotating gallery — although I do admit that I usually matte their artwork with pieces of construction paper. These construction-paper mattes are reused whenever I switch the artwork, and the mattes do add a nice touch.

If you don't have a wall for this, how about your laundry room? I don't think your children would be insulted by having their artwork hung there. After all, this is where you spend a lot of time.

Souvenir Memorabilia

Despite my hate of clutter, there is something I love about souvenir shops at tourist destinations. I don't know why. My husband hates them, so he keeps me in line and keeps my purchases to an absolute minimum, if anything at all. I am truly grateful because I know that every penny spent this way is a penny wasted. But we must have memories of our trips and vacations!

Of course, I recommend photos and videos, and I have already spoken about keeping and storing those images. But for those of you who must have more, I would recommend thinking about your Christmas tree. If your Christmas tree is like ours, it is delightfully cluttered with ornaments — so what better place to keep your souvenirs?

A lot of tourist shops have souvenirs specifically for your tree. We like to create our own souvenir ornaments by hanging a knickknack or crafting something from materials we found (like seashells). This serves two purposes. One is that we actually have a "useful," specific place for the souvenirs we bring home. Secondly, every year, as we hang our ornaments on the tree, we are reminded of that special trip or vacation, which is really what souvenirs are supposed to do. And, as an extra bonus, your Christmas tree will provide great conversation starters with guests over the holidays.

Journaling and Blogging

The old meets the new. Journaling and long letters are old-fashioned pastimes that can serve as ways to record and treasure days gone by. I know that some women do a great job keeping a journal. I am always jealous of them. In today's world, a blog is kind of like a journal, but one that is meant for others to read as well.

At one of my seminars, I met a woman who kept a daily blog about her children, with pictures and other features. She even photographed their artwork and papers. She shared all of this with the grandparents who lived far away. But what she also did that was so "Smart Martha" was that she printed the blog out for her children and stored it for them every year. It was like a detailed biography of their lives, completely illustrated.

With this type of inspiration, and my jealousy toward those who can journal, I recently started to "journal" on my calendar website, Cozi.com. It has a place to jot down a few words — every day if you like. It dates and stores the entries, and there is even a place to download photos. If you so desire, the site will also automatically send your "journal" to whomever you want, every month.

We'll see how long I can keep this up. I simply do this when I'm checking my calendar for the day. I'm hoping it makes my Christmas newsletter easier to write. If I can keep this up, I may print just one copy every year or so for our family scrapbook.

Are You Kidding Me? A Family Scrapbook, Too?

We don't have a family scrapbook just yet, but I do have a collection started. I found myself keeping sentimental letters, newspaper articles, and other paraphernalia that really did not have a place of their own. Often I'd put these in my Bible or prayer book, or perhaps in the front of a family photo album.

One day, when I was cleaning out the cupboard where I keep my family photo albums, I noticed that I had a growing collection of memorabilia like this. And to stick to my own Smart Martha advice, I had to find a place for these or get rid of them. But where? They really weren't the kids' things, so they couldn't go in their memorabilia boxes. They weren't photos, so they couldn't go in the photo albums. Finally, I decided that they were scrapbook material for our whole family, and that I would collect them in a bin until I found the time to put them into a family scrapbook.

What kinds of things am I talking about? Prayer cards and programs from funerals, obituaries of family and friends, newspaper articles that involve the whole family or my husband, programs from ordinations and weddings, and some family award certificates. I could put these away in a file, but these are archived memories that I hope to easily pull out and share with my children now and again, and not forget about them.

BE READY FOR YOUR RAIN

I hope that my sharing with you what I do in regards to keeping track of our mementos will help you to decide what you want to do with yours. There are many alternatives and methods, so you will need to look for solutions that will work best for your own family. For some, it will be over-the-top memorabilia collections and displays. For others, it may be absolutely the bare minimum. Both of these extremes have their advantages and disadvantages. Your job is to find not only what works best with your busy lifestyle and schedule, but also what fulfills the need and desire that you have to keep track of and record these memories.

It seems to me that the times when we are the busiest and most exhausted are the times when we want to have the most reminders on film or otherwise. I know this feeling. I've operated a video camera many times while nursing a baby so that I wouldn't miss a dance recital number or soccer goal. When in doubt: record, shoot, and save. Some moments don't come back. For this reason, having some kind of system for storing and saving the memorabilia will give you a method for keeping track of all of it.

So, as the saying goes, "When it rains, it pours," you will know where your buckets are. It may not be neat and orderly, but it will collect the rain that you want and temporarily store it.

I felt the "rain" when I had First Communion one day followed by baptism the next.

Mary/Martha

When done with a desire for a Mary/Martha balance, these precious moments with our families can be cherished the first time around, and then relived together again when the family album is passed about. The Mary attitude helps us to be present in that moment, and the Martha attitude helps us to physically capture the moment and store it away in a practical manner.

Chapter 7

THE HEART OF THE MATTER:

Stirring What Is True, Beautiful, and Good in Our Children

Finally, brethren, whatever is true, whatever is honorable, whatever is just, whatever is pure, whatever is lovely, whatever is gracious, if there is any excellence, if there is anything worthy of praise, think about these things.

PHILIPPIANS 4:8

As I begin this important chapter, I am reminded of something I heard speaker and author Jim Stenson say about raising children: "You've got one chance and one chance only to raise your children."

This used to scare the wits out of me. With six children at home, and three in college, it still does. "Am I doing enough of this activity?" "Am I spending enough time with that?" It is good to reflect often on Jim Stenson's statement, to see in what areas our parenting needs more attention.

I say that to you from one side of my mouth as a good introduction to this chapter — but out of the other, I want to remind you of what truly makes a difference in childrearing. It's not the ballet lessons, the karate lessons, the summer camps, the classical music you play in your home, the easy access to craft materials, the time spent in the great outdoors, or any "activities" you do with your family that make the BIG DIFFERENCE in your "one chance" to raise your child. Some of these activities can be important for your child and family, but they are small pieces of the puzzle. The most important pieces of the puzzle are you and your spouse.

Your attentive presence to your children is the real difference-maker. Nothing fares better for the healthy development of a person than close personal bonds with another human being. For children to grow up knowing that they are loved unconditionally by their mom and dad is the best thing you can "do" for them. Being able to play the flute well or knowing how to recognize a Renoir painting pales in comparison.

And if you haven't noticed by now, this really is the overarching theme of this book: an encouragement for you to order your life so that you can be present to those whom God has put there — to be more like Mary of Bethany. We want to be like Mary and really be present to our children. Look them in the eye so that they know you are there with, and for, them *always*.

"SCHEDULING GOD IN"

God should be the heart and soul of every family. There are so many books written about teaching children about God and having a Christ-centered home that I don't feel like I can even scratch the surface here. Perhaps the most important point to reiterate from the many helpful books I've read on this subject over the years is that **faith and values are better caught than taught**.

More than anything else we do for our children, or the great opportunities we provide for them, **the very best thing we can do is to be present and attentive to the most important need of our children: their relationship with God**. And if, as husband and wife, we are asking Christ to be at the center of our lives and marriage, then our children will have the greatest chance of bumping into Christ when they are with us.

Sound easy? We all know that it's not. Both of these very important points are difficult to do. There is no fool-proof curriculum for raising faith-filled kids. There's no guarantee that our children will love Christ — even if, for example, we say particular prayers, do a certain number of "religious" activities each day, and teach them from the Baltimore Catechism. Faith, after all, is a gift of God's grace, given when, and to whom, He wills. As the Gospels show us countless times, faith comes after an encounter with Christ, through which one's heart is stirred by grace to love and to follow.

More than anything else we desire for our children, Keith and I want our children to know and love Jesus through His Church. We, therefore, ask Him (at times, beg Him) to be a part of our family. We especially ask Him to be present in the ordinary routines of our life.

Here are a few of the ways we invite Jesus to be with us:

+ **Car rides:** We try to always start our trips with a prayer to our guardian angels. This helps establish the fact that angels are real, and that we each have one, whom we ask to keep us safe when we are in the car and throughout the day. On longer trips, we generally say the Rosary. When Dad taxies the middle- and high-school kids to school in the morning, he leads them in a handful of morning prayers. We know some families that say a Morning Offering on the way to school, listen to everyone's prayer requests for the day, and then pray for those requests.

+ **Mealtime:** As mentioned in Chapter 3, which discusses dinnertime, besides praying grace before and after dinner, we offer other prayers and/or devotionals during this time, generally following the indications of the liturgical season the Church is celebrating. (Just a friendly reminder to keep these devotions to an appropriate length.)

+ **Bedtime:** We have a bedtime routine that includes more than just brushing teeth and reading stories. We have a few set prayers that Dad says with the elementary school-age kids, including the Prayer to St. Michael the Archangel. I usually take prayer requests and pray for those with the kids. At times, we have also used a simple daily recollection, when we silently remember the things we have done that displeased God that day. We then pray an Act of Contrition together, telling God we are sorry for the sins of the day and asking for His forgiveness. Before the children are tucked into bed, they receive a blessing from Dad, which includes making the Sign of the Cross on their foreheads.

+ **Regular confession:** I remember one particular time when we realized that it had been over two years since one of our younger children had been to confession. We felt like bad Catholic parents. How can we keep track of our kids going to confession when we have a hard enough time keeping track of our own confession times? The answer for us was to make the Sacrament of Penance easy and accessible by going to church together every week during a weeknight confession time. While we don't make everyone go to confession, we generally insist that all go with us to church. The church where we attend confession also has Eucharistic Adoration at this time. It's a good moment for the entire family to spend a few minutes praying with Jesus, while those who want to go to confession can do so. We seldom stay longer than half an hour. And we also go out for pizza afterward. (We refer to this time as the family RAP time — Reconciliation, Adoration, and Pizza!)

+ **Celebrate the Church's liturgical seasons with attention to the true purpose of each feast or fast:** Christmas isn't when Santa

SMART MARTHA'S *Catholic Guide for Busy Moms*

climbs down the chimney, and Easter isn't when his friend the Easter Bunny comes hopping by. We can have Santa and Peter Cottontail, but they only "visit" and bring gifts *because of Christ.* Going out of our way to keep Christ at the center of the holidays also reminds us to keep Christ at the center of our homes.

✦ **Make Sunday and Sunday Mass special:** Sunday is special because it is the Lord's Day. We rest and play on this day because it is a gift from God and a promise of our eternal rest with Him forever in heaven. We attend Mass as a family every Sunday, followed by a big brunch with our favorite breakfast foods. At times, we've also read and discussed the Lectionary readings before or after Mass. We sometimes discuss what the priest said in the homily or how a current event touches on matters of faith. Family picnics, bike rides, hiking, or other activities are expected for the entire family — and dessert is a necessity every Sunday!

These are just a few examples of how we invite God to be present throughout the days, weeks, and months of our family life. Perhaps this is too much for some of you, while for others it may not be enough. Parents need to decide what their own families need. More does not necessarily mean better. Done with love and faith, these prayers and activities call us back to focus and find Christ, just like Mary. They also give us that quality time with one another, just like Mary.

FOUR OTHER IMPORTANT AREAS

Truth and Beauty Lead to God

Why would someone bother to give her children piano lessons? Or why do some families seem to thrive in the great outdoors? Why does my son's Catholic high school require service hours? Why do children of all ages love to hear a good story? The answer to these questions lies somewhere in our built-in desire to seek truth and beauty.

All humans have that desire. Can you resist staring at a beautiful sunset? These activities not only reflect that desire, but also stir that desire in our children in a positive way.

As parents, we want our children's lives to be full of truth and beauty. Why? Because when we experience these things, they bring us happiness. When children are encouraged to seek out truth and beauty, they will continue to seek these things as adults. Truth and beauty are things you can never get enough of, once you have tasted them.

(Beware: If this natural desire is stifled or ignored in children, how-ever, they may not be as likely to recognize truth and beauty as adults. Perhaps you heard about the virtuoso violinist Joshua Bell playing the violin incognito in a Washington subway a few years ago. Amazingly, very few people stopped to listen to the beautiful music. Here was a world-renowned violinist, a few feet from hundreds of passersby, playing for spare change, and nobody seemed to care because they were rushing to and fro on their way to work — nobody, that is, except children, who in some cases reportedly begged their parents to stop and listen!)

Truth and beauty not only bring us happiness as adults, but they ultimately bring us to God. Excuse me while I "go deep" here for a few sentences: The truth and beauty that we experience here on earth are merely signs that point us toward God. God is Truth. God is Beauty. Sometimes people forget that truth and beauty are signs, and to Whom the signs are pointing. What is even sadder is when people stop looking at the signs altogether as adults because of their busy lives. They will not only miss a free concert by Joshua Bell, but more tragically they often stop looking for God.

Maybe that is why most parents instinctively know that beauty and truth are very important to their children's upbringing, and why they seek opportunities for them in that "one chance" to raise them.

I have chosen four important areas where children should experi-ence more opportunities to see truth and beauty. These areas are: read-ing, the arts, nature, and service. You may be looking at my list and saying, "But what about such and such?" You are probably right to men-tion these. But I'm just giving you a short list to get you started, to get you thinking about other areas where you could add beauty and truth to enhance your children's upbringing.

READING

We all know that reading is important for our children. The amount of time a child spends reading has been correlated to great scores on achievement tests, outstanding vocabulary, and less crime, just to name a few of the advantages. I think that reading deserves a place in this sec-tion because truth and beauty can be found in the stories and facts hid-den away in books. I don't think that great statistical proof is required to convince you that reading is truly a worthwhile activity for your chil-dren to engage in.

Since this is a "management" book, I'd like to suggest that you pro-actively find ways to encourage your children to read more by making reading easy, fun, and orderly. Some of us have children who love to read. They are natural bookworms. The easy and fun part is not too hard to manage for these kids. (You've probably already done many of the things I'm going to suggest, and that is why your children are like this.) For other kids who are reluctant readers, or who simply hate to read, we really need to find ways to incorporate the easy and fun into reading.

EASY TO ACCESS (HINT: MAKE LESS FRUITFUL ACTIVITY HARDER TO DO)

By easy, I mean that it should be very easy to sit down and read. Books themselves should be easy to access, along with comfy places in which to sit down and read them. Contrast this with your video games and TV. Are these easily accessible? Unfortunately, for kids today, televisions, computers, and video games greatly detract from the time that could be spent reading. I'm not suggesting that you should have uncomfort-able furniture where you watch TV, but I'd at least make turning these devices on a little difficult. Children always choose the path of least resistance.

We pack up our Wii every time we are through playing with it. We put all the cords and remotes away in a drawer. Regarding our TV, the biggest obstacle our kids face, to keep them from plopping down and watching, is that they have to ask my husband or me for permission. This is sometimes followed by a short inquisition about homework assignments or instrument practice, or help with a chore — not every time, but enough to make them think about these things before asking.

The computer is a bigger battlefield, especially for teens. So much of their time would be spent with social networking, if we gave them carte blanche. As I suggested in the media chapter (Chapter 2), limits must be put on this time, or else it will become all-consuming for most teens. They may claim that they are really reading: "But, Mom, I am reading and writing when I'm on Facebook!" Please. It's not really reading. It's twaddle — okay for some socializing, but not for any real advancement in intellect and creativity.

Talk about "one chance" to raise our kids! Let's not blow it here by letting our children spend too many hours reading simple gab and gossip.

E-books? Now that's another story. Those can be treated the same as regular books.

GET THEM THEIR OWN READING LIGHT AND "OWN" BOOK

Once each of my children gets old enough to read chapter books, he receives a reading light for his bed. We advocate reading before bed. Each child is also encouraged to always be "in a book." If they need help finding a book, I go out of my way to get them one. And if they like a particular series, I make sure they are caught up to the latest release. Libraries are a regular weekly or biweekly errand for us. I take a survey before I go to fill any book requests. In my view, when there are young, prereading children in the home, spending time with them at the library should be a weekly scheduled event.

Besides owning shelf loads of our own books, I also have a large basket of library books in our living room. I often replenish the basket with topics that everyone — and yes, I mean everyone, including Mom, Dad, and teenagers — would enjoy. These range from *I Spy* books, to army weaponry, to forensics. If I had more girls, the basket might have books about horses, princess parties, or homemade cosmetics. Having these books next to comfy furniture makes it easier to grab a book versus turning on the TV. It also makes it easier *for me* to sit down with a child and read a book, when there are a few minutes to spare.

FUN

The more that kids find reading enjoyable, the more likely they are to do it. And it seems that the more kids read, the better they get at it and the more enjoyable it becomes. I have had to struggle with some of my boys when they were just getting into chapter books, particularly my slower-to-develop readers. It seemed like such a chore for them to read. If they would just get to be better readers, I knew they would start to enjoy it. But getting to that point meant more reading and more struggles.

For those reluctant readers, I really go out of my way to find books that they are interested in. For one really, really, slow reader, I used one of the recently released Harry Potter books. We even went to a 24-hour discount store at midnight to purchase it. For another child, I bribed him with: "If you read the book, I'll take you to see the movie at the theater." And often, sequels to movies are available in book form and greatly appeal to children.

We've experienced wonderful family time with books that my husband has read aloud. He is currently reading the Redwall series to our 5-year-old and 9-year-old. He does this for about half an hour before bedtime, usually three or four times a week. Listening to books on CDs in the car has also encouraged the kids to reread the books on their own or continue reading in the same series.

Experts say that seeing Mom or Dad read has an influence on how much a child reads. Do your children see you reading, and enjoying it?

I'm not sure if this fits under "fun," but in the summer I offer reading time to earn video-game time. The formula I usually use is three hours of reading earns one hour of video games on a non-video game day. We also participate in summer reading programs at our library that incentivize reading by offering desirable prizes for reading a certain number of chapters or hours.

ORDER

(a) Keep All Books in One Place

I tend to think that books can look untidy, especially if they are like ours, with covers often missing from old paperbacks. And I've also noticed that kids have the worst time putting books back on shelves.

One way that we've contained our book mess is to keep all books in one room. For us, it happens to be our schoolroom, which doubles as my office. It could just as easily be in a den. I've had books in our game/toy room before and didn't like the extra mess and cluttered look they caused in there. The exception to this "rule" of keeping all books in one room are the books that the kids are currently reading. These and any "special" or "favorite" books are allowed to be kept at their desks in their rooms.

(b) Order for the Library Books

We also have a special place for library books. "Mine" — or really, the family's library books — are in a big wicker basket in our living room. I have also developed a system for my children's individually chosen library books to keep them from getting lost or forgotten.

Each child (ages 5-12) has his own library bag. Attached to the bag is each kid's library card, so it never gets lost. In theory, the library books must either be in the bag or in the child's hands, nowhere else. When they are done reading a book, it goes right into the bag. Most of the kids keep their bag hanging on their bedposts so that they can look at the books before bed. If they want someone to read some of these library books to them, they simply bring the whole bag down and follow the same rules.

By following this system, you can see that it is less likely that any library books will get lost or mixed with the books that you own. Of course, the kids often forget to put them back in the bag, and sometimes they've even lost the whole bag!

Two of my children have used inexpensive canvas bags, which we

Our library books.

purchased from a craft store. We had a lot of fun decorating them with fabric paint and stencils. This ready-to-go bag comes in handy when I have to run a quick errand, attend a meeting, or go to the doctor's office. The kids can grab this bag to read in the car or during the long wait.

I also have the rule that they can only check out as many library books as can fit in their bag. I've heard that some moms have the rule that you can only check out as many books as your age. That makes sense, too.

(c) Paperback Book Order

We have accumulated many paperback kids' books, the ones with no readable spine. These are hard for kids to look through when they are all packed together on a shelf. I have found that plastic storage baskets can hold these together, look neat on a shelf, and facilitate finding the book you want, as well as making it easy to put the book away.

Paperback books are easier to access in a basket like this.

(d) Establish "Reading Times"

Establishing a nightly quiet study time during the school year has helped to encourage both studying and reading. During this time, there are no electronics on, except for the people writing papers or doing research. This has helped to establish a regular reading time for the younger children in our family who don't have the homework assignments like the older children. It also keeps them quiet and less distracting to the students who are working. We have a flexible start time for this. It begins when the dinner chores are done and goes until bedtime on weekday nights.

When I had all young children in the house, I established what we called "FOB." I stole this title from a summer camp that I had attended as a child. It took place for about an hour after lunch. This stands for "Flat On Bunk" (or "Back" or "Bed"). During FOB, babies and toddlers would nap. Those too old to nap, also had to go to bed. They had to be completely silent and stay in bed for one hour. Of course, that library bag would come in very handy here, or they'd grab other books from our own library. Often, they would draw or journal.

This time was really good for the kids. It gave them a much-needed rest and down time, to be quiet and do a little creative thinking. And you can imagine the break it provided for me!

(e) Too Many Books Are Clutter

I am a recovering bibliophile. I have to deny myself from going to any used-book sale. I can't even glance at the shelf of books in the Goodwill store. Several years ago I would have thought that saying "books are clutter" was blasphemous. I love books, but I've come to recognize that there is no need to store (and dust!) too many books. They are messy and cluttered looking. Exceptions are made if there's no easy access to a library; the library doesn't carry the books needed; the book is referenced often; and, of course, there are some childhood classics that you've just got to own, like *Green Eggs and Ham*.

This idea of lightening our book load is just something you may want to consider for your own home.

THE ARTS

I mentioned in Chapter 5 how important it is to slow down and not have "too many activities" for kids. When we think about trying to add "the arts" to our children's schedules, we may begin to feel overwhelmed. How we handle this with our own busy crew is to limit their schedules to just one art and one sport at a time. This was difficult for our daughter, who one year had to make the decision to give up her dance lessons to pursue piano.

Again, every family situation is different. We have made exceptions for some of our children who showed a particular talent for two different arts. Joseph plays both violin and piano. Having a family guideline such as what I'm suggesting is helpful, but what you add to your family schedule is something you need to prayerfully decide and continually evaluate.

But are lessons the only way to expose our children to the arts? Of course not. We can have art in our homes, as part of our family entertainment, and for kids to "play" with. Here are a few ideas.

MUSIC

When I was growing up, we never had music playing in our home. My exposure to music happened when I became old enough, at age 13, to buy my own 45s to play in my room or to listen to my own radio. You can imagine what kind of music I grew up on as a teenager in the 1980s: disco, funk, and then some classic rock.

By the time I got to college, I had moved on to Christian rock, as my faith was beginning to grow. And for some reason, when Keith and I got married, we decided to play classical music in our home. I remember purchasing a Top Twenty Classical Music Favorites on a cassette tape to start our collection. Now, 23 years later, my husband owns a couple thousand classical music CDs and hundreds of old vinyl records, the latter of which have, he claims, a better sound than CDs. Talk about clutter! But it's his "hobby." (Actually, he is really quite the expert.)

For our entire family, classical music has a place of importance. One of our sons is even a piano performance major in college.

We are not solely a classical music family, however. We really like all kinds of music. To illustrate this, consider the rest of our family. Our oldest son went to school to become a sound engineer. Another son plays guitar, both rock and classical. Our middle son plays both the drums (no lessons required!) and cello. And our daughter is a college student majoring in theater, where she acts, sings, and dances. We could be like the Partridge Family if only we had a funky bus.

I am often asked how I have raised such musically talented children. Next, they ask if my husband or I play an instrument. I have to say no, except in high school I played the clarinet. Keith is so talented — he can play both a CD player and a turntable!

In reflecting back on what we did and what we do now in our home, I have the following suggestions for raising "musically talented," or at least "musically appreciative," kids:

In the Home

+ Take lessons in some kind of instrument. The more you can understand music, the more you can appreciate it.
+ Play a variety of music in your home, particularly a variety of classical music. The more a classical piece of music is heard, the more it is enjoyed. Classical music offers emotional depth, intelligent structure, and form not usually found in most pop music.
+ Listen to the CDs *Classical Kids* or *Beethoven's Wig: Sing Along Symphonies* in your car or before bed. We also like Robert Levine's CD and book *Story of the Orchestra: Listen While You Learn About the Instruments, the Music and the Composers Who Wrote the Music!*
+ Let your children "play" classical music games on computer websites. Try these at *www.MusicTechTeacher.com/musicquizzes .htm*. Many major symphony orchestras also have websites for children, with games and activities. Check out the San Francisco Symphony site (*www.SFSKids.org*) or the New York Philharmonic site (*www.NYPhilKids.org*).

As Family Entertainment

+ Take children to age-appropriate concerts starting at a very young age. We would regularly attend free summer symphony concerts in the park when the children were very small. This included bringing a picnic and quiet activities for the children to do, such as coloring. One parent would often tag team the other parent for chasing the 18-month toddler around. Now our family attends a larger variety of free concerts in our city. With such a large number in our family, I scavenge our newspaper regularly for those free types of cultural events.

+ When the children get older, splurge a few times a year to see some real musical artists in concert. Seeing and hearing these masterpieces in concert played by the world's greatest virtuosos can inspire a child.

As Play

+ Besides owning a variety of instruments and a piano that are only for serious practicing, we also own an electronic full-sized keyboard that is meant for play. There isn't a day that goes by when someone hasn't sat down at that keyboard and composed their own little tune or tried to play something they've heard in a song. It's used for background music and sound effects for the kids' drama productions — and with its automatic beats, it can instantaneously transform the room into a dance party!

+ For young children, besides a keyboard, have other toddler-friendly instruments for them to play, such as drums, maracas, and kazoos.

VISUAL AND PERFORMING ARTS

Let's now consider ways to foster the visual arts and performing arts together. I'm no expert in art, so I won't even enter the debate on what is art and what is not. I go simply on what I like and find interesting. I like art that inspires, such as the work of Fra Angelico. I like art that reflects cultural or historical events, like that of Winslow Homer. I like art that is beautiful, such as Monet's. I like art that is fun, like we find in many of Salvador Dali's works. I like art that makes you wonder, like the work of Edward Hopper. If you are not very "art-orientated," then take the opportunity to study and explore this area with your family. A great place to start is an art museum. They have a variety of art forms, so you can see what moves you, what you like. Try these other ideas:

In Your Home

+ Be purposeful in choosing art in your home. I like to use themes in rooms. For example, we have one room with just Van Gogh pictures. In another, we have surrealists. I know artists are insulted if you buy or hang pictures according to room colors, but I do it all the time. There is such a large selection out there that you can easily find a great picture *and* have it match the sofa. I also use very economical prints so that I can change them out more frequently. If you are able to, there is also a lot to be said about owning a real piece of art. I'm not talking about buying a Picasso, of course, but maybe something from a local artist. This way you are supporting the arts locally, as well as being able to discuss the piece with the artist. Sharing this experience with the kids can be invaluable, especially if the opportunity arises later for a child to inherit the piece for his or her own home.

+ Dance, art, and drama lessons are available to children in most communities. See if these opportunities are right for your family.

+ Bring home beautiful art books from the library. There you will find wonderful books for children on art of all forms — from ballet, to Shakespeare, to Renoir.

+ Encourage your children to try out for the school play. Our homeschool group also puts on a play every year.

As Family Entertainment

+ Go to an art museum. I think the best advice about taking children of all ages to a museum is to make it short and sweet. I know if you pay an admission price, you feel that you have to "get your money's worth." But you'll remember the pieces much better, and have a more peaceful, relaxed time, if you just pick one or two sections or limit your time. One thing we always try to do, especially when we are visiting another city and won't have the opportunity to come back to the museum for a while, is to take a general tour. Tours highlight the best pieces, are usually one hour long, and give very interesting information. If you have a local art museum, look for those free days or purchase a membership so you don't feel as though you've got to see it all at once.

+ Go to the ballet and other productions. Again, I look for free opportunities. Many communities offer an inexpensive children's series. We see *The Nutcracker* for next to nothing every year, as well as other traveling theater productions. Our community also has "Shakespeare in the Park" for free. If you are not near a city with these kinds of opportunities, attend the local high-school productions or spend a little money to support the community theater.

✦ Watch art DVDs, available at your library. *Sister Wendy's Story of Painting* comes to mind. (Yes, this is art history taught by a wonderfully quirky nun. Sister Wendy Beckett also has other DVDs and books about art.) We also have learned a great deal from some of the children's DVDs we've watched together. We liked the *Dropping In* series. Our library has *Dropping in on Rousseau*, *Dropping in on Matisse*, and *Dropping in on Picasso*.

As Play
Making Your Own Art

Children love coloring, painting, pasting, sculpting, carving, etc. This is such good constructive play for them. Why don't we allow it more? I'll tell you why. It's messy. It's not easy to store. It creates clutter. It is not easy to get out or put away the material. It sometimes destroys things — tell me you haven't had marker scribbled where it doesn't belong. These are my problems I have with art and craft materials. What are yours? We are all such Marthas!

Now, since we are trying to be *Smart* Marthas, we can look back over the list of problems and see what we can do to encourage this kind of activity, *but* solve or lessen some of our problems. Here are some ideas to make life with art supplies easier.

First, I decided to keep all of the craft-type material in one place. For each of us, this is going to vary by our storage options. Some of us don't have very much storage space to spare, and some of us don't really need to have too much space devoted to this.

Depending on the ages of your children, you may want the craft storage to be out of reach of the small children. I especially keep markers out of reach of toddlers. As I mentioned, I've been "burned" too many times. Sharpies are like arsenic in our home, kept under lock and key.

Our craft supplies are in a cabinet over our laundry room sink.

Once you decide on a space, then you need to sort, clean out, and replenish what you have. Remember to keep similar things together. Make things easy to access and easy to put away. Use clear bins or label them. A little organization and maintenance go a long way. Once you've got a place like this, your craft material will seem to just beg to be used.

Another helpful tip is to keep the craft activity in one "safe" place. Ours is always done at our kitchen counter. If anything spills, both the counter and the floor can be easily wiped clean. I still always insist on having newspapers down when painting.

Since most of our craft material is not easily accessible for the small children, I have to take the time to get it out for them. This makes it easier for me to keep it in order, and also ensures that expensive or harder-to-use materials aren't wasted. Since not every moment is a Play-Doh moment, having to ask me to get it for them helps me keep Play-Doh from ending up in the carpet or in the sofa. My philosophy is: "If you are old enough to get the craft materials out, you are old enough to put them away in their proper place."

It seems as though I always have exceptions to my rules, and so I have one here. I do keep crayons, paper, and coloring books in an easily accessible place. These things are away from babies and toddlers, but not from 4-year-olds and 5-year-olds. The kids don't need to get me if they just want to color. To keep crayon cleanup easier, consider having only a dozen crayons available to kids this age. As they get older and want the 64-crayon box, they will also be old enough to keep all 64 picked up.

We have a nice supply of drawing and craft books to get the creative juices flowing. It is also very typical for me to get a drawing and/or other craft-type book at the library for new inspiration. Usborne drawing books and Ed Emberley drawing books are our family's favorites.

A final note about the order, replenishment, and accessibility of your craft material: it nearly eliminates all last-minute trips to the store the night before a school project is due. If you have middle- or high-school students, I know you have experienced their panicked pleas to take them to the store to buy poster board. Despite our countless instructions about not procrastinating and always being well-prepared, our children will often need last-minute craft materials for a project. Being well-stocked in the craft department often helps provide an instant solution for: "Mom, I've got to have this for the poster that's due tomorrow! Can you run me to the store?"

That reminds me of another exception to keeping the craft material together. I keep a supply of poster boards and a couple tri-fold science boards in the back of our hallway closet. This is only because they don't fit in our craft storage area, and they are out of the way there.

Making Your Own Plays, Dance Recitals, or Operas

I mentioned in the toy chapter (Chapter 1) the importance of a costume bin. This simple bin can be filled with all kinds of costumes and props to encourage this type of creative play. After seeing a show, children often will want to imitate what they saw, and create stories and performances of their own. I remember when we went to see a circus how for the next couple of weeks, there was a daily circus performance going on in our toy room. Our circus had jugglers, clowns, dancers with scarves, and Beanie Babies that were thrown through hula-hoops.

Puppets have also been a great source of imaginative storytelling and performances. I have seen many puppet productions played out on the back of our sofa. We had a particular set of Jack and the Beanstalk puppets, which provided many variations of that fairy tale.

NATURE

I personally think that nothing reveals the beauty and awesome power of God like nature. You see His strength in the roar of the ocean; His beauty in the petals of flowers; His intelligence in the intricacies of a spider web; His infinity gazing at the stars. And don't you think that the more you study and try to understand nature, the more complicated and mysterious it becomes?

Children are drawn to nature. They love being outside. They love looking at animals and bugs and leaves and rocks. Most kids know that God made that big tree and the beautiful sunset. I think that keeping kids close to nature keeps kids closer to God.

And yes, I know that many tree-huggers deny that God exists. But that is why, as parents, we need to keep helping kids make the connection that they naturally want to make. I always try to tell my kids things like: "Isn't God amazing to make those birds able to find their way hundreds of miles back to their nesting grounds? They have a natural GPS. That couldn't happen by chance, could it?"

Many families do a great job of exposing children to nature. It's enjoyable spending time with our families outdoors, exploring God's creation. The question I'd like you to consider now is: Why don't we do it more?

I sincerely wish that our family would do more. I'd like to see us spend less time watching movies and more time stargazing. I'd like to see us spend less time playing video games and more time hiking. I'd even like to have less time at a weekend sporting event and more time on weekend camping trips. You can see from my wish list the problems that probably keep many kids from getting outdoors: video games and other media, and too many other activities.

By setting some limits on our video games, media, and other activities, we can free up some time to spend time with nature. Here are a few suggestions we have tried that may help get you and your children more attuned to nature:

+ **Plant a garden.** Get your children involved. Let them pick out the seeds, plan, and plant. They love it when the plants grow. I've never had a particularly green thumb, but we always try to have a garden. You can even use containers if you have no space. We use the raised-bed gardens because they are smaller and easier for this busy mom to manage. Our 5-year-old, Gabriel, took a great interest in our gardens this year. He was in on all of the action. The great moment was when the sunflowers finally grew taller than he was. We watched the sunflowers as their "heads" turned to follow the sun throughout the day.

+ **Camping.** You knew this one was coming. Yes, it is very counter-Martha. It takes a lot of work. But there is something about the combination of all the work, being together, and nature that does something for families. We've done our share of camping over the years — and most of it when the children were young. We always kept thinking how easy it would be to camp when the children got older — but now that they're older, it's so difficult to fit it in between sports' schedules and work schedules. Don't use having little ones as an excuse. Just do it! Start small — one night!

+ **Hiking.** This activity is inexpensive, and healthy! Go online and find all of the parks — national, state and local — that have trails. Put the baby on Dad's back and go. While you are exploring the parks by hiking, find out what other programs the parks offer. Many of these are free and very informative.

+ **Boy Scouts.** Speaking of camping and hiking, Scouting does these well. They also have a whole litany of other skills and experiences they offer. I have met so many great Eagle Scout young men that I've always hoped to have one of my own. Unfortunately, for us, Scouting was too much for our family. We made two different attempts with three of our sons, but ended up barely finishing the year both times. Circumstances weren't right for us, but they may be for you.

✦ **Biking.** Many cities are doing the "Rails to Trails" thing. Look to see if there are any interesting bike trails for you to explore in your area. You probably will need a good bike rack. Ours goes into a hitch on our van and can hold five bikes. The other bikes we carry inside the van. Of course, both Mom and Dad can carry a toddler in a bike seat on their bike if needed.

✦ **Zoos and natural museums.** Family passes are worth every penny. Most zoo passes can be used at other zoos. When traveling, we often explore the zoos in these areas. Usually they are free with our pass. Also look for free or inexpensive programs that both zoos and museums offer. If you see a program you like, register, and get it on your calendar!

✦ **Plan a nature vacation.** (1) If you always go to the beach, consider one that tries to preserve nature versus the boardwalk scene. I've also seen many programs offered at state parks near beaches that teach about that ecosystem and its creatures. Again, these are usually free. And you are on vacation. You have time for this. (2) If traveling to a vacation spot, consider staying at campgrounds or state parks on your way. You don't necessarily need a tent. Many offer equipped cabins. (3) Consider a "nature" destination. Yellowstone versus Disney, for example. Because nature is so relaxing and beautiful, usually nature spots *are* a vacation destination. Take full advantage of this when you choose your activities and accommodations. Make your activities, and even your lodging, bring you closer to nature. Consider a state park or a national park for your whole vacation. As mentioned above, they usually have cabins and many free activities.

✦ **Read about nature.** Okay, this isn't quite the same as experiencing nature firsthand — but who wants to see a poisonous snake "firsthand"? Learning about nature will help you appreciate it more, and will inspire you to study it more. There are so many beautifully illustrated nature books at your library. Make sure you bring home some nature ones from each trip. I also try to bring home the nature books that relate to what we are doing. For example, before we go to the beach, I get one about sharks — just kidding!

Actually, the books will highlight dolphins or shells, and similar topics. If we have seen tadpoles recently, we get a toad book. If the leaves are changing, a book on trees.

✦ **Get a pet.** Some pets can be beneficial for children to have. It can teach them responsibility and get them a firsthand, up-close look at animals. That being said, I don't think reptiles or rodents or any wild animals should be pets. These animals are meant to be free. I also hear that birds are the messiest pets. I guess that leaves us with just cats, dogs, and, for the weak, fish. And yes, this Martha has had rats, frogs, mice, hamsters, birds, fish, cats, dogs, and an iguana. We also have had many overnight guests, such as turtles, chipmunks, and snakes. We even hatched chicks one year.

Many of the pets we have had, and currently have, were rescued from people who no longer wanted to take care of them. This is why getting a pet is a big commitment. We can say it is the commitment of the child wanting the pet, but we all know that it is the mom who really makes the commitment. The most responsible child stills needs an adult watching over him to make sure he is keeping up with his responsibilities.

My Smart Martha advice here is to pray about it, talk about it, and then get a fish (just kidding again). Seriously, you need to know what you are getting into. Dogs take a big time commitment. I begged my friend not to get a dog. She had five small children — the oldest was 9. She wanted a dog to protect the children and to play with her 6-year-old son. She didn't listen to my advice and got the dog. My friend lasted half a year with the dog, until she finally found another family to take it from her. It was too much.

Never take in wild pets, even if it is just for a short while. We've only had overnight guests because they were injured and needed protection. Your kids will grow to respect nature if you

treat all nature with care. If your child captures a frog, put it in a container for as long as the child is interested in studying it. When this is over, usually in a few minutes, show the child how to gently let it go where it will be safe.

✦ **Use everyday teachable moments.** As with the frog example above, study it and talk about it. Point out particular birds from your window when you are eating breakfast. See if you can identify them by their colors. How about trying to identify them by their sounds when you are outside? Collect colored leaves in the fall. Find the tallest dandelion. Don't be too busy yourself to miss the beauty in nature — and more importantly, to link that to God.

SERVICE

"Love cannot remain by itself — it has no meaning. Love has to be put into action, and that action is service."

MOTHER TERESA

The same Jim Stenson who said that we have only one chance to raise our children also said this: "The sign that your son is a man is not that he can take care of himself, but that he takes care of others." I really like this saying and often repeat it to my teenage boys. When I find myself "stuck" doing all of the cleanup in the kitchen, I often complain to the kids, "Hey, can someone help?" Sometimes one of my children will say, "But that isn't my mess" or "I cleaned up what I had." This always warrants that same response from me: "A boy doesn't become a man just when he can take care of himself, but when he can take care of others." And yes, it is true that we all know many "girls" and "boys" who are in their 20s and 30s.

We've just thought about finding God in the beauty of nature. It's of even greater importance to find God in the faces of others. In fact, when we go to meet Jesus as King of heaven and earth, He will expect us to have served Him in those faces of the needy:

"Then the King will say to those at his right hand, 'Come, O blessed of my Father, inherit the kingdom prepared for you from the foundation of the world; for I was hungry and you gave me food, I was thirsty and you gave me drink, I was a stranger and you welcomed me, I was naked and you clothed me, I was sick and you visited me, I was in prison and you came to me.' Then the righteous will answer him, 'Lord, when did we see you hungry and feed you, or thirsty and give you drink? And when did we see you a stranger and welcome you, or naked and clothe you? And when did we see you sick or in prison and visit you?' And the King will answer them, 'Truly, I say to you, as you did it to one of the least of these my brethren, you did it to me.' " (Matthew 25:34-40)

Jesus continues His parable and tells the people that those who do not serve the needy are banished from heaven. He is pretty blunt about this.

We don't need to travel very far to find opportunities for service. This is the first message we want our children to learn. Charity begins with those "other Christs" that God has placed into our lives. These are often the hardest ones to serve. Husbands must serve wives. Wives must serve husbands. Parents must serve children. Children must serve parents. And the hardest of all: Siblings must serve siblings.

We can do activities and talk about this, but unfortunately for us sinners, this is another one of those lessons that is learned most from our example and practice. Sons, in particular, learn to serve their mother, and other women, from the example they see in their father serving their mother.

Since this is more a matter of how one raises children, a topic I said I wasn't going to cover, you may be wondering why I am bothering to mention service in this book. It's simply that these "Mary moments" of serving can sometimes be planned and scheduled with our "Martha methods." And when I think about all the soccer moms, baseball moms, ballet moms, and every-other-kind-of-running-around-after-our-kids moms who are spending all this time and energy with these activities, it makes me stop and wonder: What if we put some of that time and effort into teaching our children about service?

The families I know who regularly go to the soup kitchen, or pray at the abortion clinic, or make participating in mission trips for their children a priority genuinely have kids who seem to have a heart for others. In some ways, these activities are an outpouring of their generous hearts. But I also believe that these activities can generate a generous heart. They feed off one another. And just the fact that a family decides to make service a priority speaks volumes to the children.

Our family participates in many of the service opportunities offered by our church and school. We try to take advantage of these one-time deals whenever they come — things like the Giving Tree at Christmas, collecting cans for food banks, and baby showers for homes for unwed mothers.

If you have young children at home and it's hard to get out to do service work, try a child sponsorship with your family. Keep the picture of your sponsored child displayed, and pray regularly for the child. We've also had many great experiences with adopting a grandparent from a nursing home. This does not require money on your part, just time. Many of these elderly people are extremely lonely. I always find it sad that so many spend their last years on earth in this way. They especially love to see babies and young children.

We currently have a Meals on Wheels route that we do. This is an easy way to visit the elderly and provide them with food. We also have sent our children on mission work. A few attend a yearly local mission for a week that rebuilds homes for the poor and disabled in the poorest section of our city. We've also had a son participate in a mission trip to El Salvador. Many of these experiences can be eye-openers for the kids.

There are as many ways to participate in service to others as there are families. And as our family's service projects have changed over the years, so will yours. My practical advice is to (1) pray for the opportunities and (2) schedule something. Make sure that our children realize that serving others begins by serving our neighbors. Who are our neighbors? I would suggest that our primary neighbors are those who live in our homes. The next ones are our literal neighbors who live down the street and in our community. And finally, it is as Christ said: Those who are in need.

As we finish this section on service, here are just a few ideas for you think about and discuss with your family:

- ✦ Does our family do a good job of taking care of one another? Do we seem overly concerned with just doing what is required and not walking the extra mile (Matthew 5:41)?
- ✦ Does service come naturally for our family, or does it seem to go down like another work project that we "have to do"?
- ✦ "Religion that is pure and undefiled before God and the Father is this: to visit orphans and widows in their affliction, and to keep oneself unstained from the world" (James 1:27). Are there widows and widowers who need help in our own neighborhoods and families or in our local nursing homes?
- ✦ Should service opportunities take priority in our schedule? Are we doing a good job teaching the need to serve others with our current schedule?
- ✦ An experience serving others who are needy can often bring teens out of themselves. Unfortunately, though, they seem to have the

busiest schedules and no time for this. Is there a way to involve our teens in service projects or to provide a mission experience for them?

The funny thing about serving others is that it truly does bring happiness. Self-absorbed folks are miserable. I've seen teens come home from these work camps, dirty and tired, but with a joy that lasts for days. And really, could we expect anything different? If we are serving others, then we are truly serving Christ. Service becomes an opportunity to be with Christ. How could we not be happy after being with Jesus?

✦ ✦ ✦

DON'T WORRY ABOUT YOUR WEAKNESS

With our oldest son getting married this year, we have had plenty of opportunity for reflection. What could we have done better as parents to prepare him to go out into the world? What could we have done to strengthen his faith? What could we have done to prepare him for marriage? for a career?

Yes, we have had many, many regrets. We've realized many mistakes. Many things that we have learned from our mistakes I have tried to share with you in this book. (And I'm not talking about things such as putting Sharpies in drawers that young children have access to, or letting toddlers play with Play-Doh where the baby can reach it. Yum!) I am talking about the importance of time and attention given to our children. The message is just that simple!

Even as I write this chapter, my mind is spinning with ideas on how we could get more nature in, or more reading in, or more art in, and on and on. I'm hoping that this book does that for you, that it *gets you thinking*. Some of these ideas are good, and I should pursue them, but it should never be at the cost of being so busy that our family sacrifices the importance of just being together.

At the same time, I am also filled with regret as I write this chapter: Am I doing enough? Should Jacob be taking piano now? When was the last time I took the kids to a museum? This book, and especially this chapter, is *not* meant to send moms on a guilt trip.

Every one of us has made mistakes. We all have things we should have done better. But thank goodness for God's grace. If raising children completely depended on us, we'd all be sunk. We do what we can do.

I've always liked the verse where Jesus tells St. Paul that the apostle is strengthened through weakness; so instead of complaining of his weakness, St. Paul sees it as an opportunity for God to work:

> But [Jesus] said to me, "My grace is sufficient for you, for my power is made perfect in weakness." I will all the more gladly boast of my weaknesses, that the power of Christ may rest upon me. (2 Corinthians 12:9)

If you have "weaknesses" in areas of your childrearing or shortcomings from the past — and who doesn't — offer them to Christ. He can work through them. Your weaknesses will then be far more powerful than your strengths. And then you, like St. Paul, can be glad that you had those weaknesses. It gives Christ a chance to work through you.

How does one do this? Simply recognize your weaknesses and your shortcomings of the present, and from the past, and ask Christ to overcome them. We need to do this often. Raising children requires a lot of prayer.

Raising children also requires a lot of work. We've only got one chance. See what you can do to fill your family's lives with truth and beauty. Show them Who *is* Truth and Beauty. And when you've done what you can, leave the rest to God. As our parish priest always says, echoing St. Ignatius of Loyola: "Work like it depends on you. Pray like it depends on God."

Chapter 8

BABIES:

Bringing Out the Mary in Us

A SAD BEGINNING TO THIS CHAPTER

I need to begin this chapter with a confession. I don't have a baby in my home now. I almost didn't include this chapter in the book, because my "baby" is now five. When I handed in my outline of the book to the publisher, there was not a baby chapter included in the proposal. But shortly after finding out that my book was accepted and slated for publication in eight months, I also found out that I was pregnant and due to deliver our 10th child in the same month. It was one of those "Godincidences," a God-coincidence. As a result, I received an inspiration, and decided that

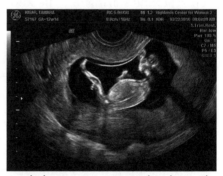

Our baby Francis, at 12 weeks, alive and kicking.

this book would be more complete if it had a chapter dedicated to babies, because babies have been a central part of my entire adult life.

I finished most of the other chapters, and the book was nearly complete. I was almost halfway through the pregnancy, battling nausea most days, but feeling remarkably better in recent weeks. Just when I was preparing to begin writing the "baby" chapter, I had my 20-week checkup. The ultrasound showed a little baby, perfectly formed, but lifeless. Our baby had died. I delivered Baby Francis at the end of April, and we buried him on May 1, 2010, the month of the Blessed Virgin Mary.

It was an intense time of pain for our entire family, but God was so good to us during this time of suffering and mourning. We felt His grace raining down upon our family in ways too numerous to mention here. How else could anyone make it through a time like that?

I still consider Baby Francis a "Godincidence," but one I don't fully understand. God was completely in charge, and He put Francis into our lives at this time, and for some great purpose, even if for only four months. For a time, I was very mad at God for choosing this path for my baby and me; but at the same time, I completely trusted in His love for me and His plan for our lives. So, needless to say, it took me a little time and courage to write this chapter.

BABIES BRING OUT THE MARY

One of the things I felt inspired to write about, when at the beginning of my latest pregnancy, is how babies can, and often do, bring out the Mary in us. Being willing to go through pregnancy and birth isn't very Martha-like. Babies take up so much time, energy, and money — not to mention that they are generally very messy. A Martha would avoid this. But there is something about a baby that encourages us to be more Mary-like, and without too much effort. Just as Mary of Bethany wanted to stay at Jesus' feet and gaze into His eyes, so mothers love just holding their babies in their arms and staring into their eyes. The housework can definitely wait for this!

CHILDREN AS BLESSINGS

When the Bible tells us that children are blessings, it's clear that God means this in several different ways. When Keith and I first became Catholic after the birth of our third child, we met an old Spanish priest who fondly told us, "Every baby comes into the world with a loaf of bread under his arms." It sounded much better in Spanish. But the point he was making is that God blesses parents with the means to provide for their children. When we have looked back at the births of all of our children, we can see very concrete examples of how this was so. My husband has had better jobs, promotions, and even financial gifts curiously coinciding with several of our pregnancies.

Another important way that children are blessings, as I just mentioned, is that they — especially babies — cause us to be like Mary. This has certainly been true in my case. Generally, I'm a go, go, go person. I don't stop. Even though I try to take my own lessons seriously, I still find it hard to slow down. But guess what happens to every woman when she is pregnant? She eventually has to slow down.

Some of us slow down right from the start — with morning sickness. Others slow down gradually, even those who are very fit. Sure, we often whine and complain about this, and we can take advantage of others who sympathize with us during our pregnancy. What is better, however, is when we truly embrace the opportunity to become more contemplative of the most important things in life, to become more like Mary. Being physically depleted, we can just sit (or lie down) at the feet of Christ and listen to Him. We can also sit and listen to our children. When I am pregnant, I try to use the opportunity to read more books to my kids and play more board games. Keith and I watch more movies together. We also talk more about what we want for our family. In fact, everything can slow down if we let it — and in the process, the most important things of family life naturally come to the fore.

Once the baby comes, we have recovery time, which is more "forced" Mary time. This time is graced with the presence of a new person. Now we really have time to take it slow, and to give our attention to this other, new, wonderful human being in our lives.

After we fully recover and are back in action, that baby still beckons us to slow down and pay attention to him. Babies wake us at night. They need their diapers changed. They need to be held and rocked. And one of the best opportunities to be like Mary: they need to be nursed. All of these actions call us to put our busy Martha schedule aside and simply pay attention to the baby.

One might think that in a Smart Martha baby chapter, I would spend the majority of the chapter suggesting timesaving devices such as baby swings and pacifiers. Not that there is anything wrong with these, but I wouldn't necessarily deem them as *Smart* Martha-worthy. A Smart Martha knows the delicate balance between being present to her baby and getting her other work done. A Smart Martha knows that she should use those Mary moments that babies present to get to know her baby — and God — better. She knows that sometimes a fussy baby or wakeful baby is an opportunity not only to be present with the baby, but perhaps also an opportunity to be present to Christ in prayer. When babies are received with this outlook — as opportunities to be like Mary and to look to Jesus — one can see a whole other way that babies are truly blessings.

And this kind of blessing doesn't end when the children are no longer babies. Children continually call us back to Christ. They call us back in joy-filled ways. They fill our lives with laughter and joy. We will take the time to look at a sunset with them or give them big bear hugs at night after we say our prayers.

Sometimes, though, we will not remember to look at Christ in the circumstances our children provide, and just get on with our busy lives. When that happens, Christ can call us to Him in "not-so-happy" ways. Look back in your life at the times you have prayed the most. If you are like me, the events that drive you to the most fervent and frequent prayer involve your children. This was true for Keith and me during the period following the recent loss of Baby Francis.

With all the joy that children bring, and their constant call for us to look to Christ, it's no wonder that the Bible considers them to be a blessing from God. This makes me wonder why any couple would want to turn their backs on God's blessings. It's analogous to locking the door and closing the shutter when the man delivering your lottery winnings shows up. It's similar to saying that we only want God to bless us one or two times, but that's all. God loves us so much, and He knows what we need. This is why I have found the teachings of the Church to completely correspond to all that I want and desire as a woman.

A TIME FOR EVERYTHING

Of course, there are times when a couple may need or desire to avoid pregnancy for serious reasons. These reasons can vary from health, to finances, to sanity. The beauty of this is that God invites us to use our freedom to decide to have sex when fertile and possibly conceive a child or to decide to not have sex at this time if conception is not desired. NFP (natural family planning) helps a couple to determine when a wife is fertile. When we find ourselves not ready to receive another child, we prayerfully use natural family planning. By using NFP to postpone pregnancy, we don't shut the door on God's blessings; we merely say, "Wait."

The moral arguments for using natural family planning versus artificial contraception are very sound and easy to understand. If you are unfamiliar with this, please take the time to study it (*www.OneMoreSoul .com* and Dr. Janet Smith's "Contraception: Why Not?" — *http://www .catholiceducation.org/articles/sexuality/se0002.html* — are great places to start). Being converts to the Catholic faith caused both my husband and I to research this topic thoroughly. After a short time, we were easily convinced that God's way meant being "open to life" throughout our whole marriage. We knew that when we weren't ready to have another baby, by using NFP, we were still being "open to life."

SMART MARTHA'S GUIDE TO BIRTH CONTROL

We have experienced countless blessings on our family when we have used NFP to either postpone a pregnancy or to conceive a child. Using an effective method of natural family planning took a little while for us to master. The best way to learn NFP is from a certified instructor (for more information on instructors in your area, please see *www.usccb .org/nfp*). But once we understood how to use the method, we wanted everyone to know what a gift this teaching of the Church is. Therefore, we took the proper courses and began instructing couples in natural family planning.

Since this is a Smart Martha book, I thought I'd share with you some Smart Martha reasons for using natural family planning. It includes some Martha benefits as well as some Mary ones:

- **It's inexpensive.** Once you've received instruction, there really is nothing else to purchase. I recommend copying your own charts or making your own on the computer. There are even software applications for doing this.
- **It's healthy.** No harmful drugs are needed. Understanding and knowing your cycle can also help in diagnosing potential problems. When nursing, it is very harmful for your baby if you are taking hormonal contraceptives. Naturally, for most women (I was not one of them), nursing will postpone the return of fertility. But when fertility does return, a woman who is using NFP will be able to recognize this change.
- **You're more likely to receive God's blessings.** This has many layers of meaning. In one way, whenever we are obedient to God, He does bless us. We can be at peace when we are right with God. In another way, there is just something about being open to God's will in our lives that makes us want to be open to having more children. People think that NFP must not be very reliable since users of NFP often have large families. Do you know how many times I've had to explain this? Yes, natural family planning works. Yes, I use it. And yes, I have nine children. Worldwide studies say that it has a user's effectiveness rate of 99 percent. This is the same as the pill. So why, then, is it that users of NFP often have more children

than those who use other methods? Because when couples use natural family planning, they allow God to work in them. They become more generous, more loving, and more open to life.

✦ **It causes couples to consider the more important questions of life, which brings them closer to God.** Every month you are faced with the same question: Do we want to conceive a child during this cycle? This opens up a whole slew of questions, which can help communication and intimacy grow between the couple. This has certainly been true for us.

✦ **Finally, it's worth mentioning that natural family planning can help couples achieve pregnancy who have otherwise been struggling.** If you find yourself or a friend in this difficult situation, I encourage you to look into NFP for moral, compassionate, and very effective help.

My heart truly goes out to those couples that have struggled with conceiving a child or have had many miscarriages. It must be a huge cross to bear when others take their fertility for granted and even complain about being pregnant. Having lost two babies myself, I can only begin to imagine what this might be like when a couple experiences this again and again. All we can do is trust.

I know several heroic couples who were not able to conceive a child. They continue to serve God and to be open to life in other ways, through their efforts as teachers, youth ministers, pro-life workers, and foster parents.

It's not completely unusual to give "birth control" advice in a chapter about babies. I've delivered in a hospital often enough to know that this is one of the questions the nurse will ask shortly after delivery. Other "baby" books include this discussion, so why not mine?

The Smart Martha model works well here in considering the options. Smart Martha knows that to be like Mary is to be one who looks to Christ. A woman completely looks to Christ when she is open to His will, which means being open to life. And yet, as a Martha, using natural family planning is very practical. It's easy, economical, and effective. Smart Martha never sacrifices doing what's right and good with doing what is easiest.

The hardest question then becomes: "Since God doesn't say I have to be pregnant as often as I can, how can I know when I should be open to conceiving or when it is time to wait?" These decisions are left to your freedom for as long as you are seeking God's will for your life.

When I was four months pregnant with this last baby, a woman came to see me, after I had given a presentation, to ask me this very question. During the presentation, I had shared that my husband and I took a "leap of faith" in conceiving this current baby. She was an older mom like me, who, by the world's standards, would be considered "done." She already had children.

Our "leap of faith" actually took a little time for us to make. Three years prior to this pregnancy, we had had another baby who died at about the same age. We named her Eva Marie. Shortly after, fully recovered from that delivery, I received an uncertain cancer diagnosis. The doctor had found a spot that could possibly be cancerous. We were told we'd just have to observe it for two years, to see if it changed in size. Throughout this time, we faithfully practiced NFP, avoiding pregnancy. When we received the cancer-free diagnosis after the two years, we continued to practice NFP.

As usually happens when using NFP, Keith and I were faced with the question: "Would we be willing to conceive this month?" It took us a couple more cycles to face that question. We considered the practical factors. Our finances were okay (we were partially paying for three college students at the time); we had a roof over our heads, and we had plenty to eat. Physically, I was in good shape (I mentioned before that I'm a dance teacher). Mentally and emotionally, maybe not — we have five teenagers! If I had waited until I was mentally and emotionally ready for a child, I wouldn't have had any. After a prayerful introspection, we realized that we didn't really have a good reason to wait any longer. So we took the "leap of faith" and gave God room to give us another child, if that was His will.

Of course, we realized that making this decision doesn't automatically guarantee a child. Conception is a marvel every single time it happens. It's never a guarantee that you'll conceive if you have sex during the fertile time. A healthy birth is also a miracle; and as we found out, it also is not guaranteed.

All I could tell that older mother was to truly pray about it and discuss it with her spouse. My experience teaches me that if a husband and wife are open to God's blessings in this way, they will never regret it. If you give your whole selves, including your fertility, to God, He will give back to you and your family a hundred times over. Of this, we are certain.

I know many couples who have lived their entire marriage being open to conceiving and not bothering with NFP. Nursing works well for them, to give them a natural spacing. Even though this is a beautiful way to live, I think learning NFP can still offer many benefits to such couples. You never know when you might have an emergency and need to avoid a pregnancy.

Another reason is just for knowledge's sake. God has given women beautifully complex systems that researchers are now beginning to more fully understand. You will have a greater appreciation of your God-given fertility. I know that learning about my cycle has given my husband a greater appreciation and respect for me and my femininity.

ESSENTIAL EQUIPMENT?

Now that we've been open to having babies, what now? Do we really need all of that stuff that comes with having a baby? It can be overwhelming to know what is really needed for taking care of these tiny blessings.

Don't get me wrong. I don't think there is anything wrong with having pacifiers or baby swings, but I don't think either one of these items makes my essential baby-equipment list. I occasionally read a blog by a woman who calls herself "Miss Minimalist." As you can probably guess, she writes about her clutter-free, simple life. In one column, she wrote about a hundred items that she lives without. She lives without coffee tables, phone books, TVs, lamps, blenders, etc.

Living a clutter-free, KISS kind of life is very appealing to me. But it's not so easy to do when living with kids. The stuff accumulation begins at birth. After having nine babies, I found that I naturally gravitated toward the less-is-more approach with each child. It really freed me up, and made our lives simpler. It made it easier to pay attention to the most important things. With that spirit, I'd like to suggest to you 18 items that I think babies (and moms) can do *without*. I've italicized the items that babies should have.

1. **Bassinets:** Although these look pretty, you are going to need a *crib* eventually, so why not just start with your crib. I'm also a fan of (gasp!) letting the baby sleep in the bed with you. Seriously, it makes nighttime nursing so much easier.

2. **Bumper pads:** For some reason, I quit using these after the fifth baby and never missed them. You do need the *crib mattress pad*, *crib sheets*, and *blankets*. When the babies were newborn and prone to soiling the crib sheet by spitting up, drooling, and wetting through the diapers, I used a *burping cloth* or smaller blan-

ket on top of the sheet for them to sleep on. When this got wet, I just switched out to a new blanket. This saved me from having to change the sheet and mattress pad all of the time.

3. **Pacifiers:** I didn't use these with my children. If the baby wanted to suck, then I simply let him or her nurse. It seemed natural this way.

4. **Baby swings:** Not that I'm against these, but it seemed as though I always had a rambunctious toddler too willing to give the baby a push. I prefer using the old-fashioned *rocking chair* for rocking and soothing the baby. Something similar to a swing, but much more portable, is the *baby bouncer chair*. (It looks like a hammock.) Although babies use this for such a short time, it can help Mom to have a few moments of completely free hands. I put mine on the kitchen counter — never too close to the edge — when I had to clean or do meal preparation. We would also put it on the table at mealtimes so that everyone could see the baby, and the baby could see all of us.

5. **Bottles:** I never used these for any of my babies. I liked the convenience and ease of nursing. Nursing has innumerable benefits for both mother and baby — but from a simply practical standpoint, it can't be beat. You tell me which is easier: sitting down and slightly lifting your blouse *or* going to the kitchen and heating and mixing (not to mention the inconvenience and expense of having to buy formula at the store) — and then when you're finished, having to wash everything and put it away. (I do know there is a very small percentage of women who can't nurse, and I'm sure this is a huge burden for them.) Nursing is a little tricky to begin with, but once you are over the initial discomfort — I know this can seem unbearable — it becomes a breeze for many women. We can complicate the whole supply-and-demand thing when we use bottles and pacifiers. If you are having any trouble with nursing, please consult your local La Leche League (*www.llli.org*) for help. They are a wonderful resource.

6. **Changing table:** When I had one for my first few babies, I used it as more of a dresser or chest. It stored not only diapers, but blankets and towels as well. I never used it to change the baby's diapers or clothes. When we moved, we got rid of it. I never missed it. I tended to change the baby's diapers on a bed, in the crib, or in the corner of our family room. I never wanted to

An example of a diaper-changing station.

bother taking the baby the whole way upstairs to do a simple change when I was downstairs. Instead, I kept a *"diaper-changing station"* in the family room. I also had one upstairs that I used at night and after baths. This diaper-changing station was a large plastic bin that held a pad or blanket for the baby to lie on, a large supply of diapers, diaper wipes, "butt cream," and a toy (like baby keys) for the baby to hold. That toy was always useful when the babies got to the age when they wanted to reach down and "help" you. The bin could slide under the sofa. Ours fit in a cabinet drawer. The "station" could also be a nice wicker basket that would sit on a shelf.

7. **Diaper Genie:** It's true that nursing babies' diapers don't smell nearly as bad as those babies who take formula. I've never really had a problem with smelly diapers. We empty our garbage frequently enough to never let them get too bad. Dealing with toddlers' diapers, however, is another story. When you get that really soiled diaper, simply put it in a plastic grocery bag and have someone take it to the outside trash. If you are not at home and have a smelly diaper to deal with, put it in a Ziploc bag. Keep a couple of these storage bags in your diaper bag for messy diapers or soiled clothes.

8. **Cloth diapers** versus *disposable diapers*: I really did try cloth for a while. But it saved only a little money, once I considered the costs for detergent, hot water, and the initial price of the diapers. I also thought that the time it took was not worth it. Store-bought wipes are convenient for both at home and on the go. I have used "homemade" wipes from a roll of Bounty soaked in baby wash. (You can search for the directions online.) *Store-brand wipes* are reasonably priced and worth the convenience. Don't use more than you need. When you change a soiled diaper, take the "one wipe" challenge. Can you clean that butt with one wipe? Hey, it doesn't take much for us moms to be entertained!

9. **Big diaper bag:** With a newborn, I usually carried around a *smaller-sized diaper bag* with all the newborn baby essentials. When my baby got past the newborn stage, I only used that dia-

per bag for all-day affairs, when I couldn't get back to my car. And often that diaper bag was switched to a backpack if I didn't have a baby on my back. I never liked hauling around anything extra. My hands were full enough. For short trips, I literally grabbed a diaper and a Ziploc bag with a couple of wipes and shoved these into my purse. Of course, every veteran mother knows to keep the car stocked with a *children's emergency supply kit* that includes:

a. Diapers

b. Wipes

c. Extra set of clothes

d. Towel or blanket

e. Sunscreen

f. Water bottle

g. First-aid kit

10. **Baby walker:** I'd replace this with an *exersaucer* instead — but if you have a safe baby walker and places for it to go, then why not? I found that my babies were very happy in their exersaucer while I worked in the kitchen.

11. **Playpen:** I never had one of these either. I liked letting the babies roam and explore where they wanted to. Of course, this does mean keeping the floors clean and vacuumed, with all the non-baby, choking-hazard items off the floor. It may also mean, as I mentioned in Chapter 1, that the older kids should keep their toys on a table. See, having a baby can mean having a cleaner house! A *baby gate* can be used to keep babies from crawling to places where they are not safe. We always had to put one at the top and/or bottom of our stairs until the children learned to safely go up and down the stairs.

12. **Pack-and-play:** I had a pack-and-play portable playpen/crib that I used a couple of times. If you travel a lot, this could come in handy. Instead, I found it easier to put the baby to bed on a quilt on the floor, rather than haul the pack-and-play around. We also were blessed to have parents who had cribs set up in their homes — something many grandparents are more than willing to do at their own expense. Usually, it's the crib *you* slept in as a baby!

13. **Plastic spill mat:** These can be nice for catching messes under the *high chair*. (If you still have carpeting or a nice rug in your dining room, then I guess this would be necessary.) We switched

to family-friendly floors in all of our eating areas when we had our first baby. By the time we think it's "safe" for us to get a nice-looking rug in our dining room, the grandchildren will probably start pouring in.

14. **Baby food, feeding spoon:** By nursing my babies past the time of their first birthday, I easily missed the whole baby-food-feeding experience. (I tried to use baby food for my first two babies.) When my babies could sit by themselves in a high chair and feed themselves small pieces of bananas and Cheerios was the time I introduced solid foods. I didn't mix baby cereal, buy expensive jars of baby food, or even mill my own. Granted, some could argue that feeding their baby is good "Mary" time. This is true. For me, however, I found that simply waiting until the babies could start feeding themselves, and nursing them in the mean-time, to be the cheaper and easier route. Good for you if you thought of using that feeding time as Mary time. Both the baby and you will now find this feeding time more enjoyable. In either case, whether you wait for your child to feed himself or begin feeding him baby food, I like the plastic "pelican" *bib*, with a trough that catches a lot of food, which simply gets washed in the sink after every meal.

15. **Baby tub:** This just took up a lot of extra space and was com-pletely unnecessary. I just used our family bathtub. And yes, it was clean enough (if someone's tub isn't, here is motivation to keep it clean). All of my babies loved to bathe in the tub from a very early age — which was just as soon as that ugly belly button thing fell off. I simply laid them on their back in about an inch of warm water, cleaning them gently with a sponge or washcloth. When they were old enough to sit up, I just filled the tub a little deeper and let them sit and play. Remember to closely supervise them.

16. **Video baby monitors:** I think the *audio baby monitors* are great. They can put parents at ease. Two of my friends have the video ones. These put parents even more at ease. I wonder, though, if the convenience of not having to go and check on the baby when a questionable noise is heard is worth the steeper price tag. But, hey, if it's a gift, as it was for my friends, then use it.

17. **Car seat/stroller combo:** These are infant car seats that snap onto a stroller. Considering that this would come in handy so few

times, it hardly makes this purchase worth it. A better investment would be a good, sturdy conventional *stroller*. The first few months when the baby is in the infant car seat can easily be managed by just carrying around the whole *infant car seat*. It fits on (or in) most grocery carts. When going to a restaurant, they're placed on a chair or on the floor. If you need to walk around a lot, then it would be worth the time to put the baby directly into the stroller. Most strollers last from when babies lie down and sleep in them until they become toddlers who sit up and crawl in and out of them on their own. I found that those small, lightweight **umbrella strollers** were easier to carry around and use in certain circumstances, especially as the babies got older and were able to walk. I had both the conventional stroller and an umbrella stroller, and used whichever one fit the occasion. With our first few babies, I lived in a city and walked everywhere. The purchase of a **tandem stroller** was definitely worth it. **Slings**, **baby carriers**, and **baby backpacks** are all great ways to keep the baby close to you or your spouse, while also allowing you to have your hands free. These are great Smart Martha approaches to taking care of your baby. The baby gets enough attention from you, but you are also able to wash dishes, grocery shop, or watch your other kids at a soccer game.

18. **Clothes that aren't soft, cotton, and one-piece:** Okay, this is slightly exaggerated. I had all kinds of clothes for my babies, but my favorites were *soft, cotton, and one-piece outfits. Onesies* are great, either as underclothing when it is cold or by themselves when it is hot. My friend, who had a baby recently, suggested using those long baby gowns for bedtime. These make it easier for nighttime diaper changes. If you've ever struggled in the middle of the night with all of those snaps, you'll know what a help this is. (I also want to use this opportunity to warn against having too many clothes.)

"KISS" WITH THE BABY

This is where it all starts. A couple adds just one small human being to their family and — pow! — they are bombarded with lots of stuff. If you can keep this under control now, it will help as the baby gets older — and when more babies, hopefully, are added to the family. Decide what you need, then store or give away the rest. (If you never plan on using something, please do not store it. Remember: Keep It Simple, Sweetie!)

A baby is a great time for a new start in clutter control. If you take these steps now, and are determined to follow them as the baby grows up, then you will be in good, clutter-free shape.

✦ ✦ ✦

BEGINNINGS AND ENDINGS

Although babies represent new beginnings, I've chosen to end our journey together here. And while this is an ending, my hope is that it will be a chance for all of us to begin again. In John's Gospel, Nicodemus asks Jesus if a man can be born again (3:4). We all must be born again, and again, and again.... This is the Christian life. And this is how it is with parenting. We start again.

I'm not saying that we all need to start over by redoing our house or by starting a new chore system. I hope there are some ideas and projects that you have gleaned from this book which will help you and your family — and you might want to start some of these. *But what we all need to do continually is start over again and again in our own lives by focusing on Christ, as Mary of Bethany did.* If we have gone a month without looking at Christ, we need to start again. If we have gone a day without looking at Christ, we need to start again. Even if we have gone only a moment without looking at Christ, we still need to start again.

So let's all be born again and look for Christ in every aspect of our lives. Let's find Him when we read to our children, when we make love to our spouse, and yes, when we are doing the dishes.

Way to go, you Smart Martha, you!

ABOUT THE AUTHOR

TAMI KISER lives in Mauldin, South Carolina, with her husband, Keith. They are the parents of nine children, ranging in age from 5 to 21 (eight boys and one girl). Besides keeping up with her kids, Tami teaches dance at St. Joseph Catholic School and drama at Our Lady of Guadalupe Catholic Homeschool Co-op. She and Keith are the co-authors of *The Incredible Gift! The Truth About Love and Sex* (Our Sunday Visitor, 1996). Tami is the founder of the Smart Martha Ministry (*www.SmartMartha.com*), and facilitates Smart Martha seminars throughout the United States.

✦ ✦ ✦

More Reviews of
Smart Martha's Catholic Guide for Busy Moms

More than anything else, today's Catholic women seek balance. Between work, home, and family obligations, it can be hard to find balance between our own spiritual needs and the very physical demands of our vocation. Enter Smart Martha — she's here to help! This practical and yet inspiring book is one part Hints From Heloise, one part Erma Bombeck, and one part wise older sister. Tami Kiser never preaches; she only shares what works for her and emphasizes the importance of balancing our inner Martha and Mary. With practical tips and spiritual support, she encourages each of us to address our weaknesses, build on our strengths, and become the joyful women God intends us to be. Whether you think you tend to be too much "Mary" or too much "Martha," this book will help you find the balance between the spiritual and the practical — and become the joyful, peaceful mother God wants you to be.

DANIELLE BEAN, *Faith & Family* editorial director
(FaithandFamilyLive.com)

Smart Martha's Catholic Guide for Busy Moms is a beautiful blend of practical wisdom for everyday life and words of wisdom to connect our faith life with our family life.
Highly recommended.

KIMBERLY HAHN, author of *Beloved and Blessed:*
Biblical Wisdom for Family Life